Always a fool for the moon, I pity the bores who refuse to swoon.

© hannah fries

© hans teensma

D0579026

© corey cusson

%8o0O@Q:

© jeff wagenheim

© amy haydon-ryan

© leslie charles

YOUR IDEA STARTS HERE

77 Mind-Expanding Ways to Unleash Your Creativity

CAROLYN ECKERT

Storey Publishing

The mission of Storey Publishing is to serve our customers by publishing practical information that encourages personal independence in harmony with the environment.

Edited by **Deborah Balmuth** and **Hannah Fries**
Art direction and book design by **Carolyn Eckert**

© 2016 by Carolyn Eckert

Storey Publishing
210 MASS MoCA Way
North Adams, MA 01247
www.storey.com

Printed in China by Toppan Leefung
Printing Ltd.
10 9 8 7 6 5 4 3 2 1

Library of Congress Cataloging-in-Publication Data
Names: Eckert, Carolyn, 1964– author.
Title: Your idea starts here : 77 mind-expanding ways to unleash your creativity / by Carolyn Eckert.
Description: North Adams, MA : Storey Publishing, 2016.
Identifiers: LCCN 2015050218 (print) | LCCN 2016005422 (ebook) | ISBN 9781612127798 (paper-over-board : alk. paper) | ISBN 9781612127804 (ebook)
Subjects: LCSH: Creative ability. | Self-actualization (Psychology)
Classification: LCC BF408 .E25 2016 (print) | LCC BF408 (ebook) | DDC 153.3/5—dc23
LC record available at http://lccn.loc .gov/2015050218

This book shows you a process for generating, developing, and refining ideas —
it's a path in three stages:

start here

gather

Accumulate
things you like,
things that
might or
might not work . . .
don't think,
just collect.
You're gathering
inspiration.

Figure out what you can keep, toss, or save for later. Break it down to move forward.

build

end here

break

Organize or assemble the parts into something new. Your idea takes shape.

* Flip to the back for the Story of the Book.

gather

TO BRING TOGETHER INFORMATION, PIECE BY PIECE, FROM AS MANY DIFFERENT SOURCES AS POSSIBLE

"I can't understand why people are frightened of new ideas. I'm frightened of the old ones." — JOHN CAGE

1 DON'T HAVE AN IDEA?

Wherever you are right now, look around you.

What interests you? What do you like?

Find something you like, and make it your own.

2

Pick One Thing

Do you find any of the light, patterns, colors, shapes, sounds, smells, or people around you interesting?

If not, how could you make one thing better?

The painter Jean-Baptiste-Siméon Chardin painted what was around the house — a glass of water, a coffee pot, a few heads of garlic on a table — and became one of the best still-life painters of the eighteenth century, while never leaving Paris, or his house.

Embroidered postcard by Shaun Kardinal

3

Don't Know What You Want Your Project to Be?

Write down what
you don't want it to be.

LEFT: **After a few years working as a radiologist, Steven N. Meyers was curious what would happen if he took X-ray photographs of flowers.**

In her book *Notes on Nursing: What It Is and What It Is Not*, Florence Nightingale writes that nursing is *not* about being a servant or about diagnosing or "physicking" (dispensing medicine) without a doctor's instructions. To nurse, she writes, "is to put the patient in the best condition for nature to act upon him," and to be "a careful observer and a clear reporter."

In 1925, Ivan Unger and Gladys Roy decided to show off their daredevil skills and played tennis on top of this biplane.

4 HAVE A CRAZY IDEA

"If at first the idea is not absurd, then there is no hope for it."
— ALBERT EINSTEIN

What is the most outrageous, ridiculous scenario you can think of?

Would it ever work?

Why or why not?

Would a part of it work?

One night Gary Dahl was at a bar with friends, and their conversation turned to caring for their pets. Dahl told his friends that he had no problems at all, explaining,

"I have a pet rock."

He decided to see what would happen if he marketed the idea, and this flash of **silly inspiration** became a nationwide craze for pet rocks. In the Christmas season of 1975, he sold millions of "pets" (complete with carrying case and manual) to a war-weary public desperately in need of something fun.

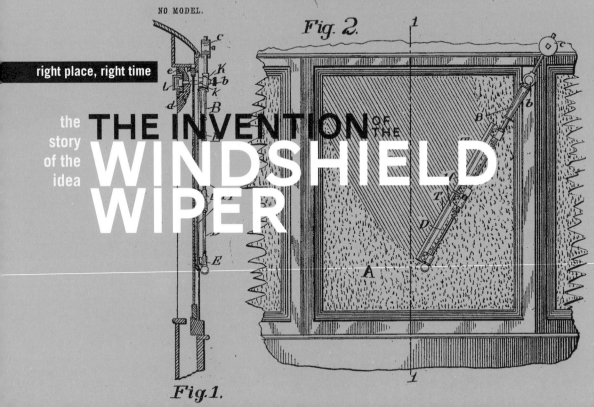

No. 743,801.

PATENTED NOV. 10, 1903.

M. ANDERSON.
WINDOW CLEANING DEVICE.
APPLICATION FILED JUNE 18, 1903.

NO MODEL.

Fig. 2.

Fig.1.

right place, right time

the
story
of the
idea

THE INVENTION OF THE

WINDSHIELD WIPER

DURING A VISIT TO New York City on a snowy day in 1902, Mary Anderson noticed that the streetcar driver was having trouble seeing through the windshield. He could open part of the window and wipe the windshield with his hand (many people at the time even used a sliced onion or carrot), but then the snow and wind would fly in, making everyone cold and wet — and he still wasn't able to see. Mary started to sketch as she rode, ultimately drawing a "swinging arm . . . to remove snow, rain, or sleet from the center vestibule-window" of the streetcar; even better, it could be operated from inside the car. Mary received the patent for her "window-cleaning device" in November 1903 and tried to sell it to Dinning & Eckenstein in Montreal, Canada, in 1905, but they responded that they did "not consider it to be of such commercial value." Her patent expired, but the idea — and need — lived on. By the 1920s, windshield wipers were being installed on every car.

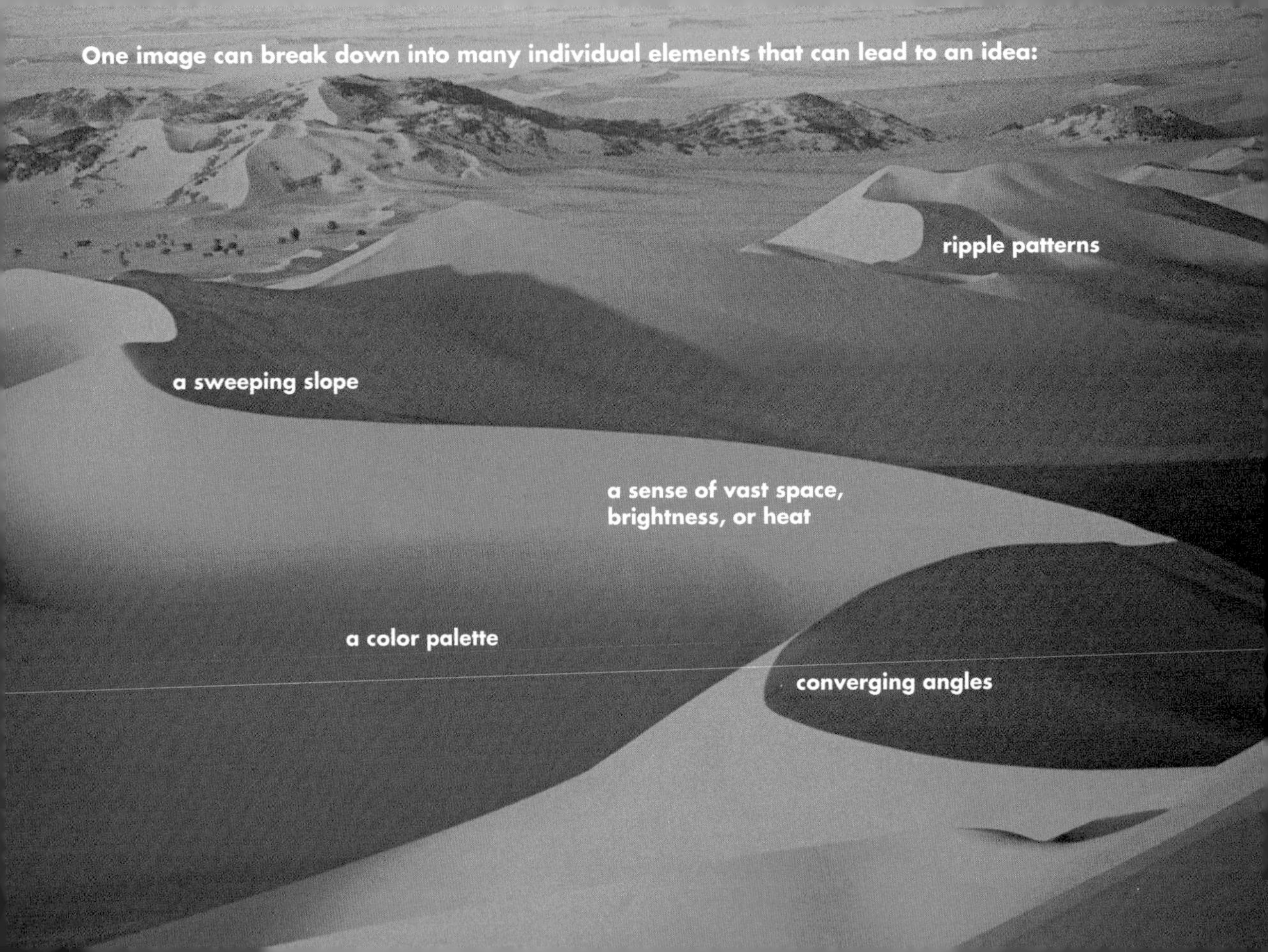

One image can break down into many individual elements that can lead to an idea:

ripple patterns

a sweeping slope

a sense of vast space, brightness, or heat

a color palette

converging angles

5

Think Like a Fashion Designer

Find a photo you like and use it as your inspiration. A photo of desert dunes was Diane von Furstenberg's inspiration for one of her spring collections, titled Oasis.

"Oasis — serene and unexpected"

— DIANE VON FURSTENBERG

Leslie Charles collects pop-tops during her morning runs. She also paints watercolor swatches and draws geometric

Be a Collector

Start gathering items you like — anything, really. They can be words, photographs, cartoons, quotes, paint or fabric swatches, patterns, sketches, or just random thoughts on sticky notes. Tack these items up where you can see them every day — all together on a wall near your desk (designers call this a "mood board"), or individually and randomly around your house so you're inspired everywhere you go. After you accumulate enough items, see if you can group them. Is there a theme developing?

got up early but my head still hurt. got a bike from the stash, adjusted the seat, put on my helmet + set off for the beach, via the back roads. got a little bit lost in the golf development: par lane, fairway street, etc. bought supplies at the art store + called myself an indulgent old lady (well there are worse things to be than a retired art student + I am not there yet!) already regret the paint purchase but not a single pencil or pen.

heard the train go by at 5:17 pm # "oh that's a sad story," said Katherine who asked about the boat full of dead plant matter. Her new neighbors "from Wisconsin" cut down the 15-foot wall of night-blooming cereus that screened the two houses. Blooms the size of platters, once a year. My mother would always have a party that night. # Also "I went to Mozambique so that I could swim with the whale sharks. And then I ..."

stayed
train 8½ pm

saw a wooden boat full of terracotta pots + dried stalks of night-blooming cereus. a bowl full of children's blocks painted gray, silver-gray + black. a compass from Concord, NH woodshop, one item in the cabinet of wonders: coral, bits of clay, can't say I saw because the sun had set (the bright pink sunset over the water) but our host Catherine described the sculpture shield made of the man screaming, sinking in his little black pond that's full up with all the metal objects she could not place. all the wood objects placed in ...

it is feb 21

night-blooming cereus

dreamed of saying No more onions — you know we have a box yay-big in the livingroom (which is true). thought about bushing out this structure to include...*(thought?) which of course gets away from the vital clarity of the charge as is. But also smell? Taste? * ate granola infused with coconut, as if I could forget that I am not in Massachusetts. * showered: there is a strong start to the day * thinking about weddings, ...

TRAIN: 7:23 a.m ___!

heard myself say I'm trying to be patient with myself but not too patient. * the clock in the dining hall seems to tick from someplace else *

Sir Ken Richardson talking about how we educate people out of creativity, increasingly moving up so that it is only The HEAD. 'Academic art like their bodies are simply a head-transport system'

observed: when Barbara says she is having terrible trouble with her ms we are not exactly happy but in the rush of sympathy also relief: we like to share our troubles, + especially those of other people (speaking of which I cannot get out of my head that an elephant fell on Indra — someway my brain processed that catastrophe) * so writing about trouble, the way to go, everyone knows it, so why UTOPIA?

feb 22 early (which is to say mainly about yesterday)

alex's meal yesterday: ravioli w/ sage butter

wintercream + berries + bits of chocolate?

Pencils! red: lavender+brown, brick red

purple + metallic orange - deft green

This red pear is twice as big as the pears at home.

7

OR

to write your notes faster, use symbols instead of words. Ever tried to use hobo signs?

(anything goes)

Write It Down!

What interests you? What is your passion? Write down random thoughts as fast as you can. Carry a notebook; keep paper by the bed, a dry erase board by the shower, scrap paper in the car, notes on your phone. Just keep collecting your random scribbles on anything you can write on. The notes might not make sense individually, but as they come together, you'll see a direction.

HOW IDEAS ARE FORMED

in an
"aha" moment

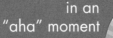

from a sudden
connection

when an
accident turns
interesting

in the right place
at the right time

8

Make a Connection

Play a game with one or two other people: One person starts by saying one word that relates to your project. Then the next person quickly says another word — any word — that relates to your word. See where five or ten rounds take you.

tree: leaf: wind: storm

tree: bark: dog: pet: fur: soft

Thomas Edison was inspired by his own work, and one thing led to another: his carbon microphone, which transmitted speech, led him to think of recording and reproducing sound with his phonograph, which then led him to the idea of viewing a fast-moving sequence of pictures with his kinetoscope, creating the first version of a motion picture.

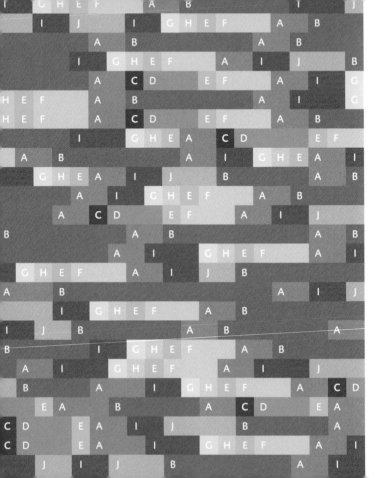

During their research on how human brains process language, neuroscienctists at the University of California, San Francisco, teamed up with designer Christian Swinehart to translate the zebra finch song into visualizations. He describes his chart like this:

"Each syllable [of birdsong] is plotted as a colored square and the sequence is read left to right and down. There is a large amount of variation but one can also see repeated motifs."

9 Research the Problem

Look up everything. What is the problem's history?
Has anything been done about it before?
What did the solution look like? Why did it succeed or fail?
Why does the world need your version?

Research can lead directly to a new idea. While researching a topic
for her doctoral thesis, Marie Curie found scientist Henri Becquerel's discovery —
that the element uranium emitted rays — very interesting. Curie decided to
investigate these uranium rays and find out what caused them. After only a few
days, she made the revolutionary discovery that an emission (which she later
called *radiation*) was coming from the structure of uranium's atom. This hypothesis,
which suggested that the atom was not indivisible after all, is considered one
of the most significant contributions to the development of physics.

born of necessity — and to avoid embarrassment

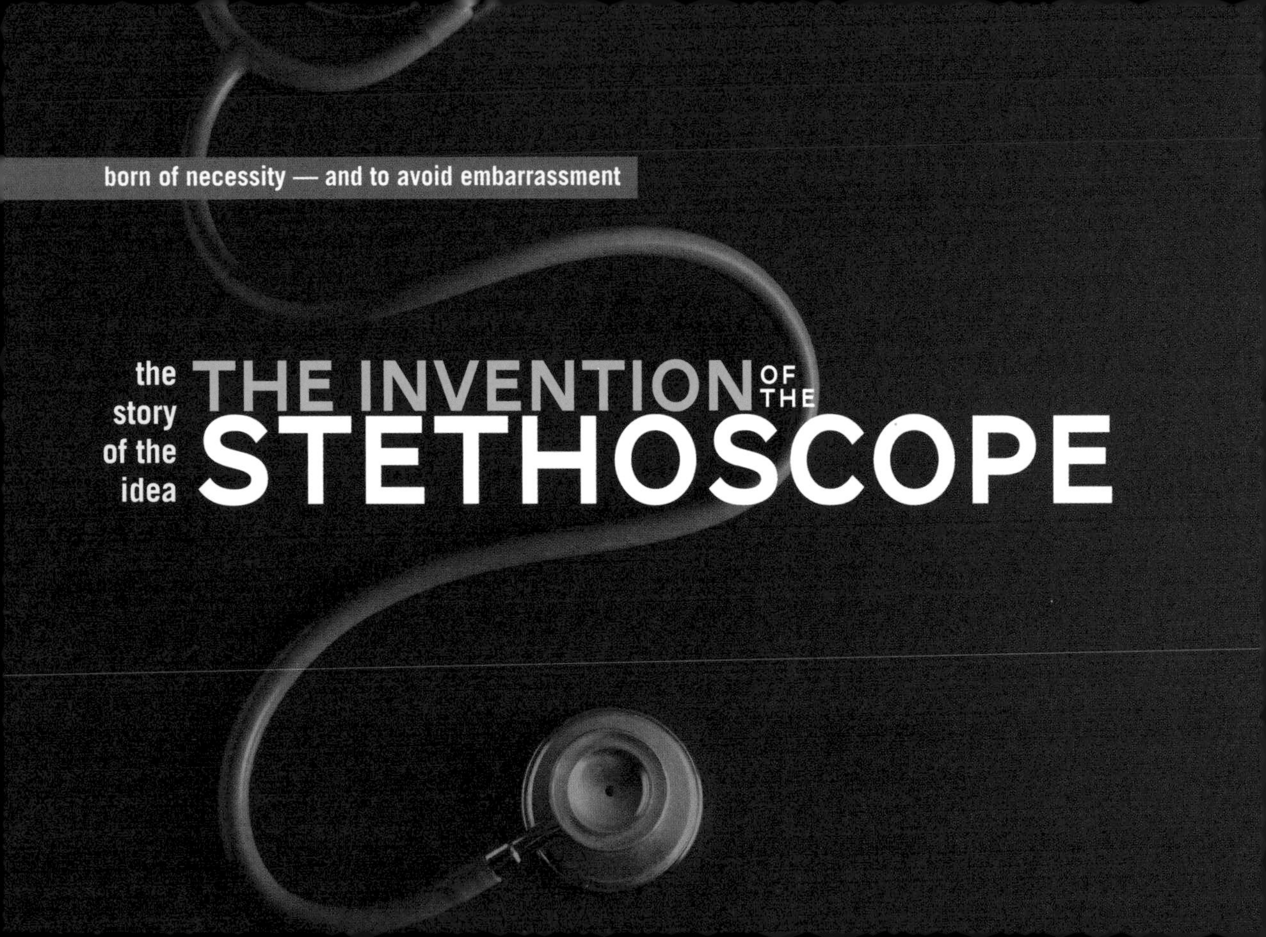

the story of the idea THE INVENTION OF THE STETHOSCOPE

IN 1816, RENÉ THÉOPHILE HYACINTHE LAËNNEC,

a French doctor, was walking in Paris and saw two children playing with a long piece of solid wood. One child would scratch the end of the wood with a pin to send a sound to the other child, who held the opposite end of the wood to her ear. Later that year, when Laënnec had to diagnose a female patient with a heart problem, he remembered the children's toy. Reluctant to use his usual method of pressing his ear and hand to the naked chest of his patient, she being an older woman (she was 40) with a "great degree of fatness," Laënnec rolled up a piece of paper into a long cylinder and placed one end on her chest and the other to his ear. He was "not a little surprised and pleased," he wrote, "to perceive the action of the heart in a manner much more clear and distinct than I had ever been able to do by the immediate application of the ear." Combining the two Greek words *stethos* ("chest") and *skopein* ("to see"), Laënnec named his new tool the stethoscope.

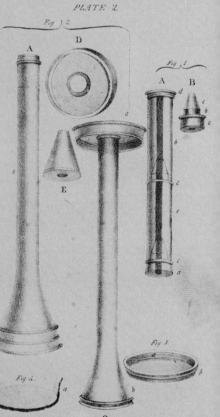

"If I say, 'Freeze, I have a gun!'
and you say, 'The gun I gave you for Christmas! You bastard!'
then we have started a scene because we have AGREED that my finger
is in fact a Christmas gun." — TINA FEY, *Bossypants*

10 Follow the Rules of Improv

Play the Yes Game.
One person says a thought
or idea. The next person
builds on that idea by saying,
"Yes! And . . ."
How far can you take one
train of thought?

11

You Can't Have It

Write down your first idea.

Sorry! You're not allowed to use it
until you think up 5 to 10 viable alternatives.
Was your first idea the best one?

LEFT:
Variations of handmade porcelain cups and plates by Dietlind Wolf

Chef Jean-Georges Vongerichten, owner of elite restaurants around the world, told Oprah Winfrey in an interview that he challenges his chefs with food he finds fresh at markets: "I found some sugar snap peas. Let's think up ten dishes. We try to think of what will turn this pea into something new."

Teresa Grow of Los Angeles's Madison and Grow designs is influenced by her time spent in Sonoma, Martha's Vineyard, and Pasadena. Each place became the name of one of her collections.

Beaded curtains, this stove, and a "bohemian vibe" inspired this wallpaper design, says Grow.

The shape of the woodstove also sparked the couch's pattern, and mussel shells inspired the pattern of the pillows.

12 Find a Detail

Find something you love the look of.

Now use one part of this thing as a reference or starting point.

If it's a building, for example, use a color, shape, pattern, or even a word on the signage. What new thing can you create using that bit as inspiration? Make an outline or infographic using the building's curved, zigzag, or parallel lines. Or make a dress with the same repetitive pattern as the windows. Or make music based on the shadows the building creates. Or . . .

13

Play to Your Strengths

Think about what you do well, and approach the project or problem through your strengths:

Are you most comfortable in groups?
Then talk about the problem with others.

Are you good visually?
Sketch out ideas.

Do you think better when you're moving?
Go for a run.

"A strong memory, concentration, imagination, and a strong will is required to become a great chess player."
— BOBBY FISCHER,
World Chess Champion

WHAT IS YOUR
KRYPTONITE?

14 Exploit a Weakness

Now approach the problem or project in a way that makes you slightly uncomfortable. Are you avoiding one line of questioning or research because it's not your usual way of doing things? If you're better at visuals, force yourself to write a list or make a phone call. If you're better at numbers, make a sketch of what this thing could be.

Doing something in an unusual way may lead you to a surprising discovery.

Despite having a speech impediment (there is a heated debate whether it was a lisp or a stutter), Winston Churchill chose to stand up in front of crowds and speak. Instead of remaining tongue-tied behind closed doors, he found he had a lot to say, especially when the Nazis were rising to power. Thrust onto the world stage as the prime minister of England during WWII, Churchill became one of the most celebrated orators of all time by confronting his weakness head on.

"Learning about the natural world is one thing. Learning from the natural world — that's the switch. That's the profound switch."

— JANINE BENYUS,
Biomimicry Institute

15

Let Nature Figure It Out

Nature's systems, patterns, and colors can lead to answers. A coating for ships' hulls was designed to be like shark skin to prevent algae and barnacle growth. The principles of echolocation used by bats can also be used to teach the blind to ride a bicycle and to help robots maneuver.

Look at a leaf, a pinecone, a rock, a toad, a shell, a sunflower, or a cat or dog. What do you see that you didn't see before?

Engineers designed a solar cell that mimics the folds and wrinkles of leaves and found it produced significantly more energy than cells with flat surfaces.

Nov. 21, 1961   G. DE MESTRAL   3,009,235

SEPARABLE FASTENING DEVICE

Filed May 9, 1958   4 Sheets-Sheet 2

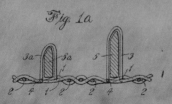

Fig. 1a

Fig. 2

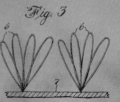

Fig. 3

the
story
of the
idea

THE INVENTION OF
VELCRO

loops

AFTER COMING INSIDE FROM A WALK in the Swiss mountains in 1948, George de Mestral noticed cockleburs all over his dog and his pants. De Mestral was curious and took the burr to his microscope. When he looked in, he noticed that the seed pod was covered with tiny hooked spines, which had clung to the loops of his pants fabric. De Mestral decided to try to replicate this natural system. After a few years of trying, and trying again, he found that nylon hardens after being heated under an infrared light; then it can be cut to form tough hooks like the burr's. De Mestral combined the words *velours* ("velvet") and *crochet* ("hook") to call his fabric Velcro.

hooks

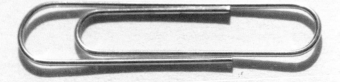

"It was invented in 1899. It hasn't been improved upon since."

— SARA GOLDSMITH, slate.com

16

Think Like a Minimalist

What is the simplest way to proceed?

Can anything be taken away?

WHAT ELSE COULD IT BE?

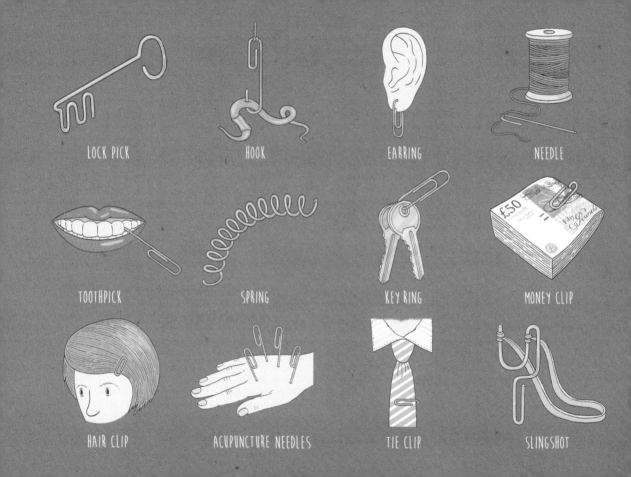

LOCK PICK

HOOK

EARRING

NEEDLE

TOOTHPICK

SPRING

KEY RING

MONEY CLIP

HAIR CLIP

ACUPUNCTURE NEEDLES

TIE CLIP

SLINGSHOT

"Most broadly, ensō represents the vast qualities of the universe, conjuring up its grandness, limitless power, and natural phenomena. But ensō can just as easily represent the void, the fundamental state in which all distinctions and dualities are removed."
— AUDREY YOSHIKO SEO,
Ensō: Zen Circles of Enlightenment

念々神通

"When a line is alive you feel the breath of the artist as well as the breath of the brush."
— KAZUAKI TANAHASHI

ensō

The Zen Buddhist practice of painting a circle with a single brushstroke as an expression of an open mind and the body's response.

17 Look to Other Cultures and Traditions

The world is a big place. Look (or go!) somewhere you haven't looked before. In the early 1850s, the people of Europe became enchanted and then obsessed with all things Japanese: textiles, ceramics, paper fans, woodblock prints, and more. The term *Japonism* was coined to describe Japanese-style works made in Europe and the United States. Claude Monet, the famous French Impressionist painter, fell in love with this new Eastern aesthetic. He started collecting Japanese prints and eventually built a Japanese-style water lily pond in his garden at Giverny — which (you know where this is going) became the inspiration for his famous water lily paintings.

Frank Lloyd Wright fell for Japan too: he loved that Japanese culture itself seemed to be a work of art — every man-made object and human action were joined as one. After touring the country for two months in 1905, Wright returned to Oak Park, Illinois, and designed his first commission, Unity Temple, inspired by the Taiyu-in-byo shrine in Nikko.

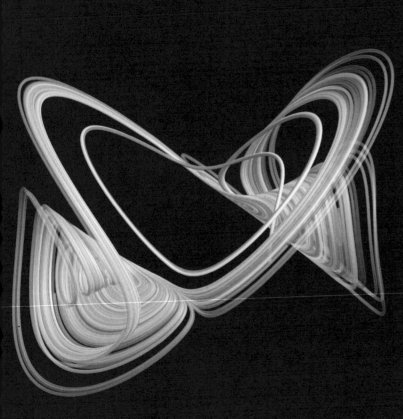

Each year, Princeton University's Art of Science exhibition calls for submissions of images produced during scientific research. According to their website, "Art of Science spurs debate among artists about the nature of art, opens scientists to new ways of 'seeing' their own research, and serves as a democratic window through which the general public can appreciate both art and science — two fields that for different reasons can feel threatening to the non-expert."

This first-place image from Christophe Gissinger (at the time a postdoctoral researcher in physics, now assistant professor at École Normale Supérieure in Paris, France) shows the chaos and geomagnetic reversals of the earth's polarity — "during a reversal, the magnetic field changes shape (from dipolar to quadrupolar structure), rather than simply vanishing."

18

Look to Other Fields of Study

Sometimes another profession can help.
A chef can look to a chemist, a toymaker to an
architect, or a snowboarder to an aeronautics
engineer for ideas to improve his or her work.
Glider controls, invented by the Wright brothers,
allowed planes to fly in three dimensions.
Their "roll, pitch, and yaw" controls have
been used by every other machine that moves
through air, space, and water freely —
including spacecraft, submarines, and robots.

"Without struggle, no progress and no result. Every breaking of habit produces a change in the machine."

— GEORGE GURDJIEFF, philosopher

Change Your Routine

Nothing new can come from a monotonous routine. Take a different route, walk on the opposite side of the street, eat something different for lunch, wake up an hour (or three) earlier, wear a color you never wear. Do this for a week. Did anything change? Does anything seem different?

In a Stanford commencement address, Steve Jobs told the audience, "I have looked in the mirror every morning and asked myself: 'If today were the last day of my life, would I want to do what I am about to do today?' And whenever the answer has been *no* for too many days in a row, I know I need to change something."

brain

PROS

Brainstorming is great for discussion
and generating new thoughts.
Something you say might spark an idea
in someone else.

It's also great to do by yourself:
Go somewhere quiet.
How many ideas can you
write down in one minute?
Five minutes? Fifteen minutes?

storm

CON

Sometimes the loudest person —
not the person
with the best idea —
has the most influence
on the group.

Brainstorm Light

20

Meet with one or two other people and talk about the problem or stumbling block. Just talking through the idea out loud can reveal possibilities you had dismissed, overlooked, or never would have considered. At the very least, it could lead you to the next logical step in solving the problem.

"It's a social function to have an idea.
In conversations you get ideas and you draw on history, you draw on your culture.
This sort of Beethoven-y individual, an isolated genius — that's not how ideas happen."
— RANDY COHEN, former writer for
David Letterman's *Late Show* and creator of the Top 10 List

BRAINSTORM
BOLD

21

Meet in a big group. Set the rules: Make a time limit for the session. Decide to make no decisions. Write down every idea, no matter how small or silly.

OPTION 1:
Each participant brings one idea on a strip of paper and puts it in a bowl upon entering the room. Read these first.

OPTION 2:
Each participant writes down five ideas and submits the list to a moderator. Ideas are read aloud anonymously. The top three ideas are chosen according to which get the best reaction from the group. Break into small groups and work with the three ideas to see if they can be taken further.

When A. A. Milne started to write stories for his son, Christopher Robin, he found it natural to use as a setting the place he loved to walk near his home in England. Ashdown Forest's Five Hundred Acre Wood became the beloved Hundred Acre Wood, where Christopher Robin and his stuffed animals became the characters of *Winnie the Pooh* and had adventures big and small. Here is Poohsticks Bridge, photographed by Craig Williams, who also walks in Ashdown Forest.

Create a
Sense
of Place

Everyone is influenced by where they grew up or where they live. How can you give your idea an authenticity of place? Can you bring elements of your surroundings — landscape, cityscape, seascape, river, or alley — into your work? Projects become richer if ideas spring from a genuine source.

Painter Georgia O'Keeffe was inspired by the objects, landscape, and architecture of each place she lived. In a letter from northern New Mexico to her husband, Alfred Stieglitz, in New York in 1929, she wrote: "When I got to New Mexico, that was mine. As soon as I saw it, that was my country. I'd never seen anything like it before, but it fitted to me exactly. It's something that's in the air, it's different. The sky is different, the wind is different."

FAR LEFT: *The Ten Largest, No. 7, Adulthood, Group IV*, 1907;
LEFT: *The Ten Largest, No. 3, Youth, Group IV*, 1907, both by Hilma af Klint

Perhaps you might look to other dimensions for inspiration. As a teenager, landscape and portrait artist Hilma af Klint started participating in séances and exploring automatic drawing. In 1904 Klint had a spiritual experience in which she said a spirit named Ananda began to guide her hand as an artist. Her style became more abstract and geometric — years before the self-proclaimed "first abstract artist," Wassily Kandinsky, painted his first nonrepresentational work in 1910.

23

Get Personal

Think about your struggles or successes and how they've influenced you. How can you translate these experiences into your work? Will successes take the form of an inspirational ballad and dark times start your "black period" paintings, or will you make it more interesting than that?

Marshall Mathers (Eminem) was looking to get famous with a mainstream radio hit when he released his first album, *Infinite*. It didn't happen. People thought the production quality was too rough, his songs were too derivative of other rappers' better work, and he had no real point of view. Because of this flop, Mathers got mad and depressed, and his friends told him to get real. In Newark, New Jersey, he went into the studio to record with Outsidaz and turned himself into his "evil alter ego," Slim Shady, filling the studio with very personal lyrics and rhymes of rage about growing up poor in Detroit.

24

Get Emotional

Use your feelings for inspiration. Are you feeling quiet, overwhelmed, or fantastic right now? Try to record that emotion in a visual way each day, each week, or every once in a while.

On a calendar, a wall, or a board, tape a paint chip, draw a smiley face, or just black out each day with a marker to document your light or dark mood. Or, for something a little more high-tech, try Cesar Kuriyama's *1 Second Everyday* app and make a one-second "mood movie" of how you feel. Film yourself every day for a week, or a month, or the rest of your life — one second at a time.

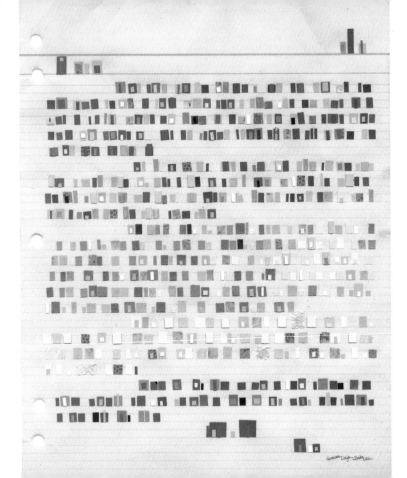

Try reorganizing that pile of papers into something else. Here, Catalina Viejo Lopez de Roda writes letters by replacing words with colored papers. What do you think she is saying in this piece titled *Letter to My Sisters*?

Shuffle Papers

Mix up the papers lying on your desk, and write down the words that first jump out at you. Or look at the materials scattered around you. What can you make, draw, or write about with what you see?

"A great deal of creativity is about pattern recognition, and what you need to discern patterns is tons of data. Your mind collects that data by taking note of random details and anomalies easily seen every day: quirks and changes that, eventually, add up to insights."

— MARGARET HEFFERNAN, entrepreneur, author, and keynote speaker

"Well now, one winter it was so cold that all the geese flew back-ward and all the fish moved south and even the snow turned blue.

Late at night, it got so frigid that all spoken words froze solid afore they could be heard. People had to wait until sunup to find out what folks were talking about the night before." — "BABE THE BLUE OX," *MINNESOTA TALL TALES*, RETOLD BY S. E. SCHLOSSER

26

Make the Ordinary Extraordinary

Exaggerate or reimagine everything you see.

Now, go a little further. Have you gone far enough?

Start by making a spoon into a fish with a long tail,
a city bus into a medieval invader, or a pen into a futuristic
portal for oxygen in an uninhabitable environment.
Or try using hyperboles to write a tall tale.

IS IT . . .

AN ARROW?

A CHICKEN FOOT?

A CROSSBOW?

INSPIRATION FOR A PATTERN?

OR JUST A COOL STICK?

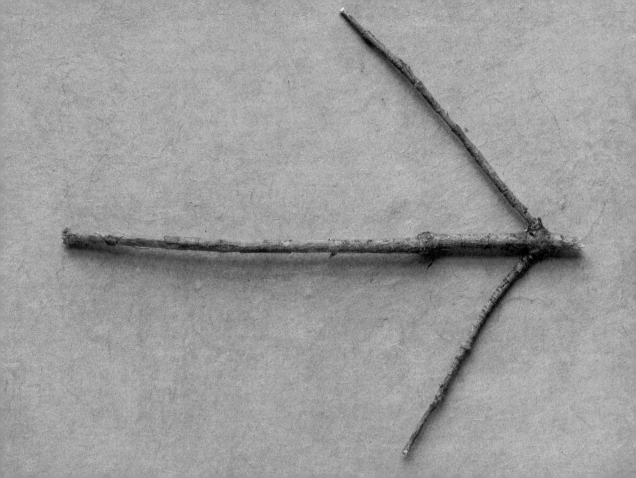

When Alfred Heineken visited the beaches of Curaçao in 1960, he saw empty beer bottles everywhere, and it gave him an idea. He hired Dutch architect N. John Habraken to design a glass brick — later called the WOBO, or World Bottle — that could be stacked to build houses.

27

Turn Trash into Treasure

Can you use something that no one else wants?
Maybe it can be transformed into something else.

Extra foam backer rods made for construction
projects became wacky noodles for swimming.
An old moldy Petri dish led to the development
of penicillin. Army-rejected parachute strap
webbing was used to design the Knoll Risom chair.

What can you do with someone else's garbage?

Peel back layers and uncover what is most important — the heart of the problem.

28
What's the Gist?

What is the one thing this project needs in order to survive? What is its most basic nature, the quality or qualities that make it what it is? What is the essence of the problem?

Rip a paragraph out of a magazine, or take the text from an email you just received. Start crossing out extra words with a pen or marker. Don't think about nouns and verbs; just keep eliminating words that are unnecessary to the meaning of the paragraph. Can you get the meaning from one sentence? From a few words? How low can you go?

Don't Overlook the Obvious

Sometimes the answer to your problem has been there all along — you just have to look in the right places.

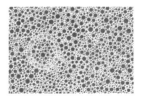

After many frustrating months, Alan Turing's decryption machine, Bombe, still wasn't able to break the German codes generated by their machine, Enigma. Then Turing realized there were "cribs," or common phrases that occurred frequently in daily messages, such as statements from weather operators ("the weather for tonight") and the ubiquitous sign-off, "Heil Hitler." By searching for combinations that produced these common (obvious) phrases, Bombe could then use them to crack the code.

LEFT: The circle and star might seem obvious, but maybe not. If you have red-green color blindness, you probably won't see the red star, and the card might even look exactly like the one above.

(Model.)

No. 398,984.

R. J. SPALDING.
FLYING MACHINE.

Patented Mar. 5, 1889.

5 Sheets—Sheet 2.

Fig. 2.

30

Think Like an Optimist

Try what Harvard professor and social psychologist Amy Cuddy has studied: Stand in a Superman/ Wonder Woman pose — hands on hips, feet apart, head held high. Just two minutes in this pose can give you more power and confidence in whatever you do next.

There is only success ahead. Daniel Kahneman, winner of the 2002 Nobel Prize in Economic Sciences, said that progress is driven by "delusional optimism" — if people had known the odds against them, they might not have tried at all.

"Stop worrying about the world ending today.
It's already tomorrow in Australia."
— CHARLES MONROE SCHULZ, American cartoonist

WHAT IS YOUR
SUPER POWER?

"Imagine if we could measure the universe using just our hands, or if we could taste a strawberry only with the feeling of our skin. . . ."
— ANA YAEL, Illustrator

THE POWER OF
SUGGESTION

Something is not what it seems.

Yps a Ekil Niart

Train Like a Spy

While sitting in a restaurant, on
a train, or at your desk, close your
eyes briefly (if it feels dangerous,
you're doing it right), and try to
remember details from all the people
around you. Who is sitting where?
Who is wearing what colors?
What is each person doing?
Open your eyes, and check to see
how you did, and then try again.
Pick one unusual detail to remember
about each person to make it easier
to place everyone in the room.

EVEN A LITTLE PAINT CAN FOOL YOU.

In the artwork above and on the previous spread, Felice Varini uses an anamorphic illusion — a visual distortion of space to confuse the viewer's sense of what is 2D and 3D — to trick your eye. Were you fooled?

32 Take a Second Look

Sharpen your keen observation skills —
just like Agent 711 of the Culper Spy Ring did to win the Revolutionary War.

When the war moved from Boston to New York, George Washington (Agent 711) needed more intelligence in order to keep a watchful eye on the British. He needed to get sneaky. Under his command, Major Benjamin Tallmadge recruited groups of soldiers and civilians to pass intricate messages regarding enemy activity in plain sight of British soldiers — by using the codes from the Culper Code Book or by hanging laundry a certain way or even by using invisible ink. These creative tactics prompted a defeated British officer to report, "Washington did not really outfight the British. He simply out-spied us."

break

**TO TAKE
A STEP BACK,
SORT, ASSESS,
DISCARD,
AND PERCOLATE**

"The air is full of ideas.
They are knocking you in the head all the time.
You only have to know what you want, then forget it,
and go about your business.
Suddenly, the idea will come through.
It was there all the time." — HENRY FORD

THAT'S A STUPID IDEA

If someone had told you he was going to sell millions of little clay figurines that would sprout a green mat of vegetal hair, would you have believed him?

An early doubter of the radio asked, "Who would pay for a message sent to nobody in particular?"

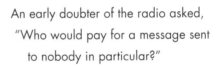

33

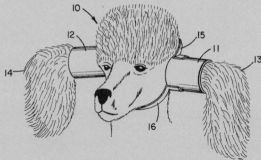

James D. Williams "Animal Ear Protectors"
U.S. Patent No. 4,233,942, Nov. 18, 1980

ABOVE RIGHT: B. B. Oppenheimer "Fire-Escape"
U.S. Patent No. 221,855, Nov. 18, 1879

So What?

Sometimes the worst ideas
open up doors for the
best ones. They can
also inspire a good idea
in someone else.

How might someone
improve your stupid idea?

by accident

the
story
of the
idea
THE INVENTION OF THE
POTATO CHIP

WHILE WORKING AS A CHEF at the Moon Lake House in Saratoga Springs, New York, in the summer of 1853, George "Specks" Crum was getting frustrated. A very picky customer kept sending his plate of French fries back to the kitchen, saying the fries were too thick. Crum finally got angry and decided to give the customer the hardest, most inedible fried potatoes he could make, so he sliced the potatoes paper thin, fried them until they were rock hard, and poured on the salt. Crum was shocked when the customer declared the dish delicious. But now he had a new hit dish, later called "Saratoga crisps."

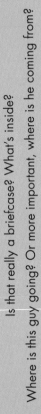

Is that really a briefcase? What's inside? Where is this guy going? Or more important, where is he coming from?

34   Ask Questions

Be a reporter. Sometimes you'll be surprised by what people tell you. At the beginning of the project, asking the right questions will usually give you a way forward and sometimes even solve your problem for you. Most of the time, a clue to what you need to do will come from one of the answers to your questions.

While researching the Mob world for his book *The Godfather*, Mario Puzo said in *The Godfather Papers and Other Confessions* that he spent hours asking the dealers and pit bosses questions between bets at the roulette wheel at the Sands Hotel in Las Vegas. When the pit bosses found out he wasn't a cop or investigator, they and the dealers started talking to Puzo — as long as he kept betting.

DO THE OPPOSITE

Tired of touring, their music, and themselves, the Beatles turned themselves into something new: Sgt. Pepper's Lonely Hearts Club Band.

35
Stop Whatever You're Doing

If you were aiming for high-end, aim low.

If you were using blue, use orange.

If it's square, make it round. If you zigged, zag.

Turn your project upside down or backwards.

Does it make things better or worse?

Do you notice any flaws?

eminal nerve have been most disappointing and do not
hile procedures in the treatment of this condition. First
ust be recognized that by and large migraine occurs in a
neurotic people with a characteristic personality profile.
igent, ambitious, energetic people. Most of them are "per-
can not tolerate carelessness, imperfection, inaccuracy in
associates or their servants. The world and its people being
ch people are uncomfortable much of the time, and under
nervous strain than affects the rest of humanity. An under-
own personality is important to them. Directive or un-
psychotherapy are often therapeutically successful. Very
stration of some mild sedative, such as phenobarbital 1/2
) two or three times a day, is often helpful to them. Many
ill be found to be doing two jobs instead of one. Women
business in the day time and take care of their family and
. They must be taught that for them such overactivity and

One thing can make you think of another: Let your reading and your experience weave together into something new.

which the patient might be sensitive mus
ite of all effort on the

36

When he was seven, Chuck Jones read Mark Twain's *Roughing It* and was struck by Twain's depiction of the coyote as poor, friendless, a "living, breathing allegory of want." He found the animal so fascinating that many years later this description became Jones's inspiration for his Warner Bros. cartoon character Wile E. Coyote.

Read Something Totally Unrelated

The more different, the better — Brontë, pop culture magazines, science research, a crime novel, a Scottish Highland romance — anything, really. Something you read will suddenly connect to your project and show you how to move forward.

WANT TO REALLY SHAKE IT UP? Go to your library and check out the first book someone returns while you're there. Read at least the first 50 pages.

Don't throw it out
if it still works!
Here's a *jugaad*
solution from India.

37 Limit Your Options

Sometimes having a lot of resources to work with gives you too many options or makes your solution too easy . . . or lazy. In India, people enthusiastically pursue *jugaad* — a term for creatively solving problems with whatever they have conveniently at hand. Don't have a bicycle handlebar anymore? A car steering wheel will do. Need to cool two rooms at once with one air conditioner? Attach a pair of pants and put one leg in each room, and you've done the trick. Tata Nano, the world's cheapest car, is their crown jewel of *jugaad*.

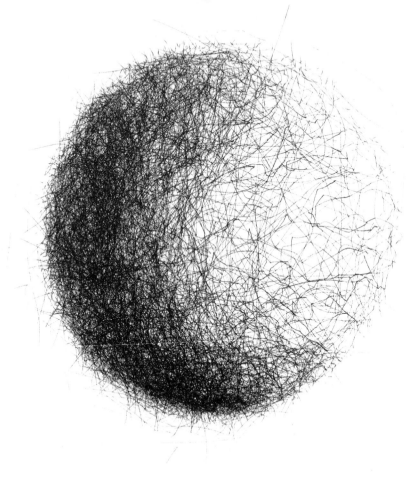

What if you just let the wind (or a leaf) do all the work?

In 2005, Mark Nystrom became intrigued by the patterns made by a fluttering oak leaf stuck in the snow. When he returned home, he wanted to recreate what he had seen, so he "cut some plastic bottles into different shapes and tied each one to a stick in the snow." Then, "wanting a more permanent record," he "constructed an apparatus to suspend a pen outfitted with sails over paper." This drawing, *Winds, November 29, 2005, Mansfield, Massachusetts, Process.2005.01*, is a record of wind conditions for that day.

The most creative work can come from the most strict limitations.

TRY GIVING YOURSELF SEVERE RESTRICTIONS:

WHAT IF you have to make an outfit using only supplies from a hardware store?

WHAT IF you have only three hours to make it?

WHAT IF you could use only three tools to build a house?

USE ONLY three notes for a music composition?
(John Cage's *4'33"* has no notes at all.)

USE ONLY one color for an interior design project?

Can it be done?

Try it, and the process will reveal to you what you really need.
Tip for success: pick a theme, time limit, or color palette.

original form   deconstructed form   new (improved) form

Deconstruct

Take apart what
you're doing
and consider the
pieces. What are
the best parts?
Get rid of the rest.

In Peter Heller's book *The Dog Stars*, he deconstructs paragraphs. Most of his novel is written in simple sentences and sentence fragments, sometimes with a paragraph consisting only of the word *and*. But the style conveys emotion, tells the story, and gives you just what you need.

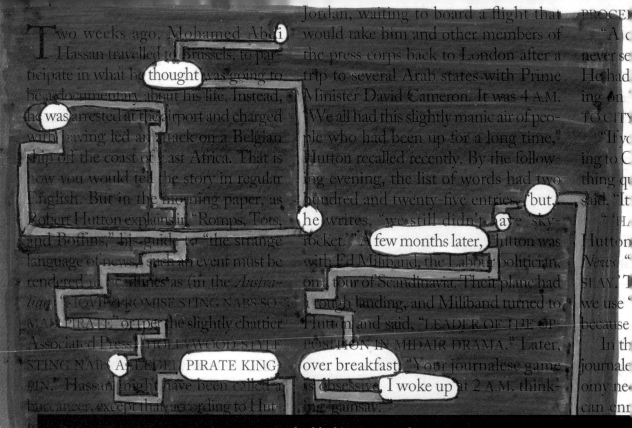

"erasure" poetry — create your own poem by blacking out text from an existing source

GIVE IT A WHIRL:

Pick a paragraph out of a magazine.
Try to present it three different ways:

1

- write
- it
- in
- a
- list

2

cut it apart
and tape it together
in a new way

3

or just black out
any words
you don't like . . .

the
story
of the
idea

COCO CHANEL AND THE
CHANEL SUIT

When Gabrielle "Coco" Chanel entered Austria's Baron
Pantz Hotel elevator in 1925, she immediately noticed
the elevator operator's uniform. She liked the man's short
coat and soon adopted the style for her ladies' collarless
(and now classic) jacket. Coco loved the style and flow
of menswear and pursued this idea of freedom of movement for women. She brought black out of mourning, put
pants into the mainstream, and helped women out of the
corset age in comfort and style.

HMMM . . .
THIS
ISN'T
WORKING

The first time Jerry Seinfeld went onstage at a comedy club, it didn't go too well —
he was jeered off the stage. It wasn't that the jokes were bad — it was all about the
delivery, the execution; the next night, he killed it.

39

Not Getting the Idea Across?

What is the main problem?
Is it the idea or the execution?

What is missing?
What does it need?

Find two or three friends and try playing the surrealist game Exquisite Corpse. Fold a piece of paper in thirds, and take turns drawing part of a character without looking at what's been drawn before.

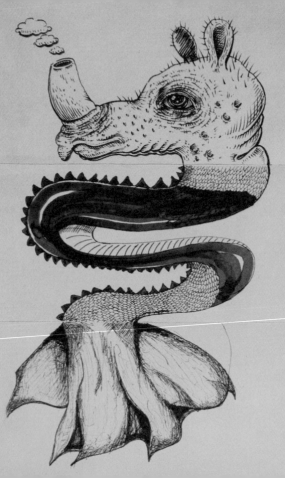

40

Rearrange and Restructure

Maybe you have everything in the wrong order.
What if you put the last thing first?
Move the middle to the end?
Whatever you do, don't start at the beginning.

Pretend you're Quentin Tarantino. In his movie *Pulp Fiction*, instead of showing the story in a linear form, he uses a circular structure: the beginning of the movie is actually the end chronologically, the middle of the movie is the beginning, and the end picks up again at the beginning. Got it?

DRUMSTICKS

BOOKMARK

COCKTAIL STICK

FIREWOOD

CHOPSTICKS

SHIP'S MAST

ARROW

MAGIC WAND

MUSTACHE

KEBAB STICK

FLAGPOLE

SWORD

Accidental photo
taken while checking
messages before driving

41

Screw Up

Sometimes the accidental becomes interesting.
Something placed upside down, a missing a piece, text copied and pasted into the wrong location: a mistake or mishap can lead you somewhere unexpected.

Accidents happen.
Look at what is left behind:

- Spill a drink on a piece of paper? What shape is the stain?

- Type the wrong address into Google Maps? Go somewhere by mistake.

- Spend the day taking random photos without ever looking at the camera or phone — at the end of the day, see what you've got.

Instead of regretting a mistake, look again; it might be better than your original plan.

"I have meant what I have done. Or — I have often meant what I have done. Or — I have sometimes meant what I have done. Or — I have tried to mean what I was doing." — JASPER JOHNS

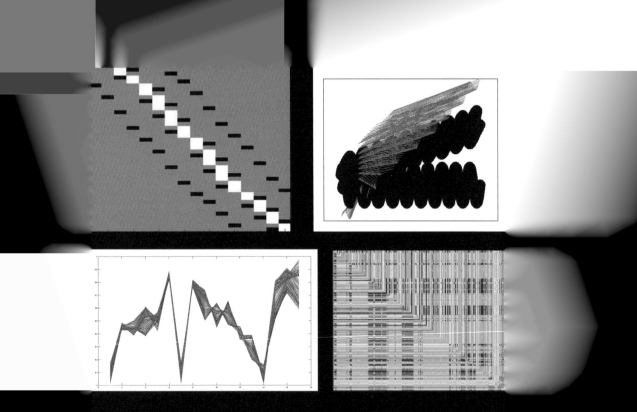

...y of the beautiful data-input mistakes made by Sam Gershman, a neuroscientist, while he wa...

42

Now Screw Up Like a Scientist

Engineers use a process called *iteration* when working through their design problems. Instead of following a process from start to finish, they might take two steps ahead and then three steps back.

TRY IT:

- Design.
- Test.
- Realize the problem.
- Step back to the problem area.
- Modify the design.
- Repeat.

By modifying the problem area and repeating the process, you can get gradually closer to a successful result.

"Science, my lad, is made up of mistakes, but they are mistakes which it is useful to make, because they lead little by little to the truth." — JULES VERNE, *Journey to the Center of the Earth* an accident turns interesting

the story of the idea THE INVENTION OF THE SLINKY

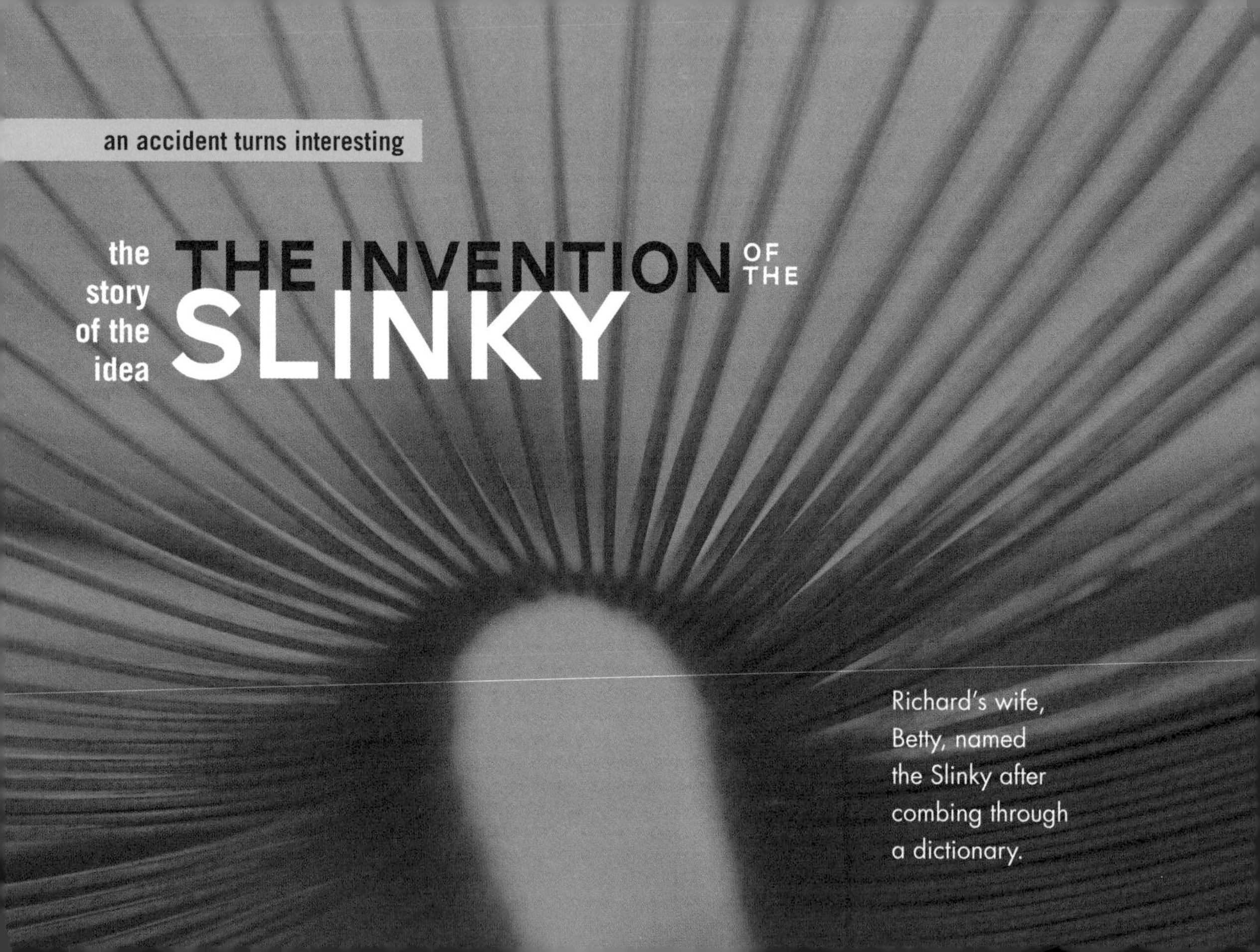

Richard's wife, Betty, named the Slinky after combing through a dictionary.

In 1943 while Richard T. James, a naval engineer, was working with torsion springs to stabilize equipment at sea, a spring accidentally fell from a shelf. It flipped end over end, "walked" with a bounce, then coiled back up. Richard was intrigued and spent a year tinkering with types of wire. He and his wife knew they had something good when the toy was a hit with the neighborhood kids.

"Everyone knows it's Slinky!"

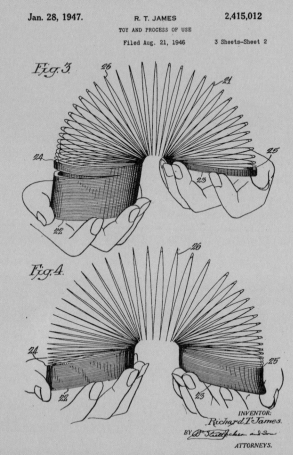

Jan. 28, 1947.   R. T. JAMES   2,415,012
TOY AND PROCESS OF USE
Filed Aug. 21, 1946   3 Sheets—Sheet 2

Fig. 3.

Fig. 4.

INVENTOR:
Richard T. James.
BY
ATTORNEYS.

WHO WOULD YOU ASK?

43

Get Honest Feedback from Three People

If you don't like what you hear, ask questions. Talk it through. Maybe there's something small you could do that would completely change their reaction. Or maybe there's a bigger problem that needs fixing.

HERE'S THE TRICK: It all depends on the right three people. Be forewarned: most people bring their own personal preferences to the table . . . they might not like yellow, and that's why they don't like your yellow project.

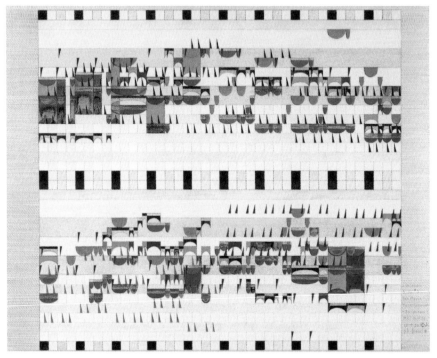

John de Cesare's drawing *Transcription of "Ave Maria"* from 1956 shows music translated visually in an art deco style.

44

Try Mozart

Use music to create a Zen moment for ideas. Alfred Tomatis, a French physician, found that more than any other composer (and regardless of a person's preference), Mozart "calmed listeners, improved spatial perception, and allowed them to express themselves more clearly."

...OR JUST LISTEN TO WHAT YOU LIKE BEST

Particular kinds of music can work for different kinds of thinking: pick the right music, the right volume, and the right moment, and the work will almost do itself. Familiar and ambient music lets you be more focused because you know what to expect; your brain isn't surprised by how the music changes.

When thinking about the feeling you want to convey with your project, how do you imagine it would sound? Would it be loud or soft? Dreamy, grand, or harsh? Try to keep your project's "soundtrack" in mind — it will help you maintain the tone you are going for.

For this poster, designed for the Automobile-club de Suisse in 1952, Josef Müller-Brockmann exaggerated sizes and angles in order to make a dynamic visual impact.

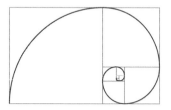

Try following the proportions of the golden ratio . . . you'll always be right!

Shape/Size/Proportion/Color

Maybe something is too big or too small.
Maybe the size relationships are wrong.
Try making the big thing small and
the small thing big. Or maybe you need
a more radical juxtaposition of scale.
Changing the scale between two objects
can change everything.

While trying to get the best sound on his phonograph, Thomas Edison experimented with many shapes for the horn: "round, square, angular, thin, short, squat while others are curved and as long as six feet tall."

Shift Your Perspective

Maybe you need to look at the problem from a new angle — from above, below, upside down, or askew. Try taking photos with nothing in the center, only on the sides. Or try one whole week of shooting only from above your head or from a worm's-eye view.

Or think like someone else for a while. Look at the problem from the perspective of different people you know — a more analytic friend, a more sensitive friend, a child, or even a fictional character, like a pirate.

For people with a neurological condition called synesthesia, the senses are unusually intertwined. For example, musicians as diverse as Itzhak Perlman, Duke Ellington, Pharrell Williams, and Billy Joel are known for associating colors with different musical tones, timbres, or keys. The composer Franz Liszt flummoxed his orchestra with instructions like, "O please, gentlemen, a little bluer, if you please!"

GO ABSTRACT:

Can you close your eyes and assign a color to a sound you hear?
What does a smell look like?

In his novel *All the Light We Cannot See*, Anthony Doerr describes how the character Marie-Laure, who is blind, sees everything in color in her imagination. Her beloved papa takes on different colors depending on whom he is talking to or what he is doing — olive green when he's speaking to a museum department head, bright red during his cooking attempts, "an escalating series of oranges when he speaks to Mademoiselle Fleury." And "he glows sapphire when he sits over his workbench in the evenings."

Australian Aboriginal artists use the style of "Dreamtime" painting to depict the stories and knowledge passed down to them from their ancestors. In his painting *Carpet Snake Dreaming*, Toby Brown Tjampitjinpa tells the story of the Carpet Snake traveling from the rock hole site of Alcootha (the center circle) west to Yuendumu and then back again to search for a fellow countryman with whom to share some food.

Look Back

What style of art, fashion, design, or architecture inspires you the most? Which period would you choose to live in if you could? What elements of this style or era can you use as a base for your project?

Our Founding Fathers were clever. When they drafted the Declaration of Independence and the Constitution, they looked back at a collaborative structure that already worked — the Iroquois Confederation. Six different tribes had united with one voice, yet they remained separate entities. The United States government was formed using many Iroquois principles, including the importance of the pursuit of happiness, which became one of our three "inalienable rights."

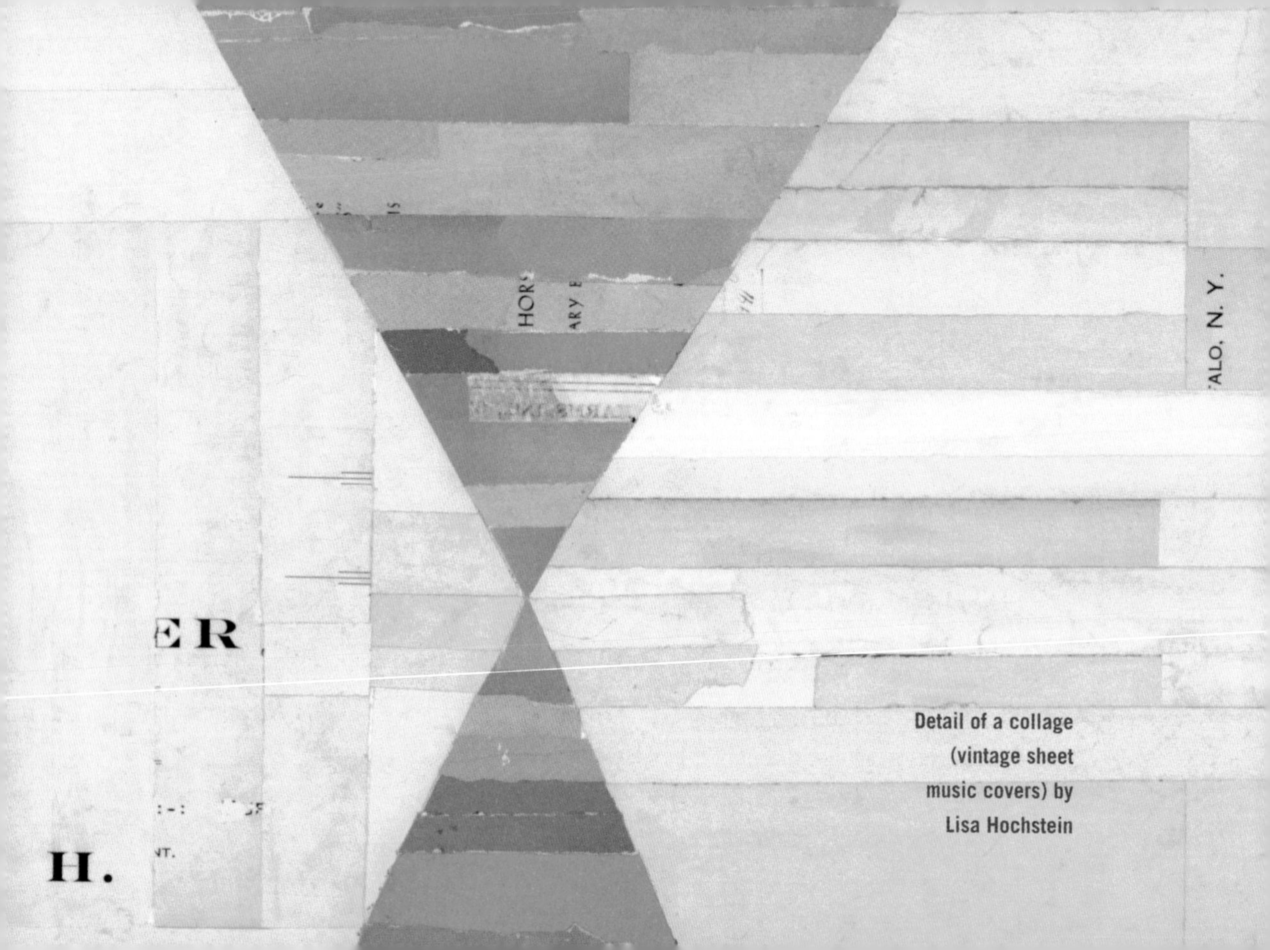

Detail of a collage
(vintage sheet
music covers) by
Lisa Hochstein

48

Talk with a Friend

But don't talk — just listen.
Even if she only talks about her day,
something she says could suggest
an answer to your own problem.
Or, if you can't help it, tell your
friend about your problem,
but listen to see if your friend
has a different take on it.

Even Einstein needed to talk it out. Once, while trying to make sense of recent experiments and results from other scientists, he went to Switzerland to visit his friend Michele Besso and brought his "struggle" with him. Einstein left after a day of long discussions, and when he visited again the next day, declared to Besso that he had solved his problem. Newly inspired, he developed his special theory of relativity.

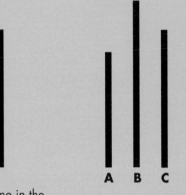

Which line in the
group to the right matches
the above line?

The Asch Conformity Experiment

In a series of experiments conducted in 1951, Solomon Asch asked 18 trial groups
the above question. In 12 trials, 7 actors in the group would give the
wrong answer aloud first, then the actual subject of the experiment would have to answer last.
Asch found that one third of these subjects would give the same wrong answer
even though they knew it was wrong — just to go with the flow.

49 Maybe You've Been Talking to Too Many of the Same People

There is a big wide world out there with all kinds of different people with many different backgrounds and experiences. They might be able to help you. Start saying hi to random strangers — the plumber, the butcher, the bus driver, the farmers' market guy — and start asking them about themselves. One of their answers might jog a memory loose or create a new connection in your mind.

Trans-Plant No.7
by Susanna Bauer

50

Share Your Idea

. . . or give away a great idea
you don't need. Someone else
might make your idea better or
come up with a new idea based
on yours. Go for good karma.
It will come back around.

WHAT IF

EVERYTHING WAS A LITTLE DIFFERENT
FROM WHAT YOU EXPECTED?

You will smile in one hour.

That thing that happened last night? Forget about it.

A year from today a new friend will impress you.

Tomorrow afternoon will be bright.

In two weeks you will find something lucky.

You will discover a new favorite color tomorrow afternoon.

You will eat the best meal of your life next week.

You will be a better person after tomorrow afternoon.

The next coin you get will be your lucky coin for life.

Tomorrow you will forget something.

Your next fortune cookie will make more sense than this one.

Just walk away and don't look back.

51

You Might Have to Kill Your Darling

You had a great idea, and it was promising, but it's just not working. It's the wrong shape, constructed the wrong way, or just isn't right. You will have to kill this darling idea before you can move on to something that works. Sorry.

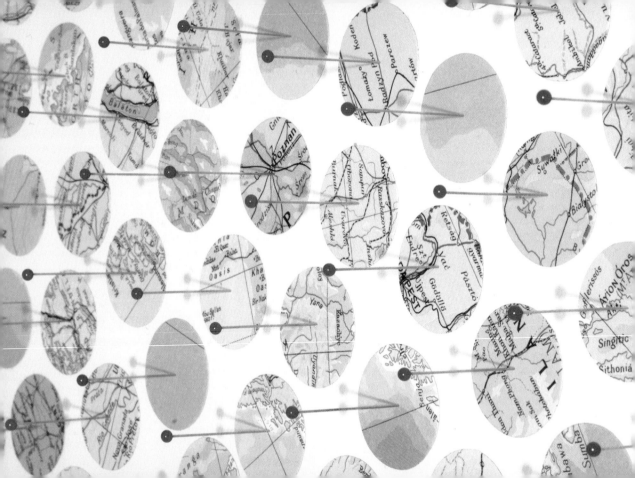

52

Stuck?

LEFT: **Artist Shannon Rankin explains on her website that she uses the "language of maps" to explore patterns and connections. Here's a detail of her piece** *Germinate.*

Stop. Now start again at the end of the problem. What do you want to happen that isn't happening? The "stuck" moment is inevitable . . . but you can get past it, if you're up for the challenge. You have to look, evaluate, and dig and feel around in that dark place to determine a way forward. There's always a way in — but it may not be easy to find.

Maybe you could walk a
little more artistically, like
Jim Denevan. Walking miles
on the beach with a rake,
Denevan creates very large
intricate patterns meant to
last only till the tide comes in.

53

Take a Walk

Stop thinking and just walk. As you walk, notice color combinations (ugly or beautiful), graffiti, trash, street signs, or characteristics of the landscape. Thoreau, Nietzsche, and Kant were all fans of long walks, which helped them clear their minds for more creative thought.

Try walking someplace you've never been before (or just never walked to before) — a coffee shop, a store, a bar, or another part of town — and find one thing of interest you wouldn't have seen if you hadn't gone for a walk.

"Silence is the
sleep that
nourishes wisdom."
— FRANCIS BACON

Silence by
Brian Powers

Space Out

Let your mind
go quiet.

Give your brain
some space.

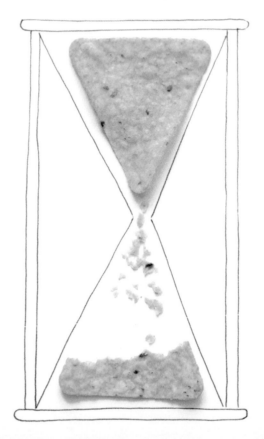

Dorito egg-timer by
Javier Perez

55

Now Wait

. . . for coffee, for a train or bus, for concert tickets, or just stand in a line. Don't look at your phone or a book. Just stand, observe, eavesdrop, or simply be. See if you go through the three phases: self-conscious, bored, and then totally fine and curious. People-watch and play the "what's their story" game. Try to figure out people's profession, family situation, or life story just by observing how they act. Or look at everyone's shoes and pick your favorite pair, or count how many people are wearing the same color. You'll be surprised (and a little sad) when the wait is over.

Dan Cobley, an executive at Google, has explained that their cafeteria lines "are intentionally kept long . . . because we know people will chat while they're waiting. Chats become ideas, and ideas become projects."

"When you work on a problem continuously, you can become fixated on previous solutions. . . . Taking a break from the problem and focusing on something else entirely gives the mind some time to . . . let the old pathways fade from memory. Then, when you return to the original problem, your mind is more open to new possibilities — eureka moments."

— DAVID BURKUS,
Harvard Business Review

56 Take a Break

Really — it's time to go do something else.
Anything to switch your mind off this project.
Your brain has to power down and start up
again later.

In a study at the Center for the Mind at the University of
Sydney, Australia, Sophie Ellwood's team of researchers
found evidence that a group who took a break and did
a brief unrelated task while working on a project generated
more ideas than the two teams who worked continuously.

Laurie Frick's brain is very busy while she sleeps. Using a sleep-tracking headband, she's collected data for almost 1,000 nights of sleep and transformed it into art. She writes, "There is a definite pattern, with much more activity than you'd imagine. It's ragged with shorter bursts of deep and REM sleep than I thought."

57

Go to Sleep

You may think staying up all night banging away at something will help, but Russell Foster, a circadian neuroscientist, says that sleeping at night enhances our creativity. Sleep lets the brain work with all of the new jigsaw pieces it created during the day, giving it time to "make associations with what you previously experienced and what you might anticipate in the future." It will help to sleep.

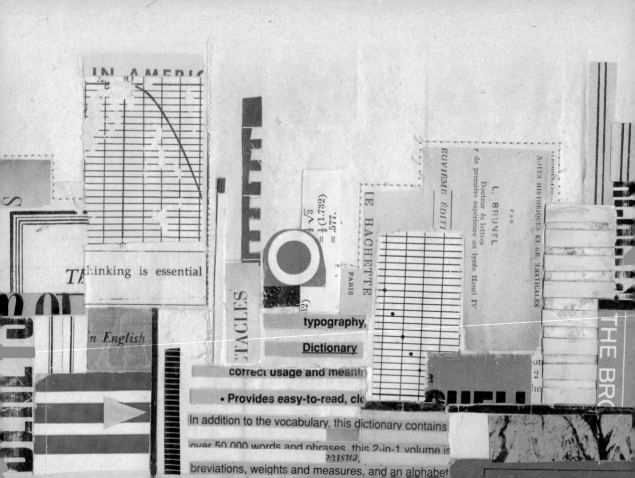

build

"It's going to be hard. But hard is not impossible." — CHUCK PALAHNIUK, author

onnection to a previous experience

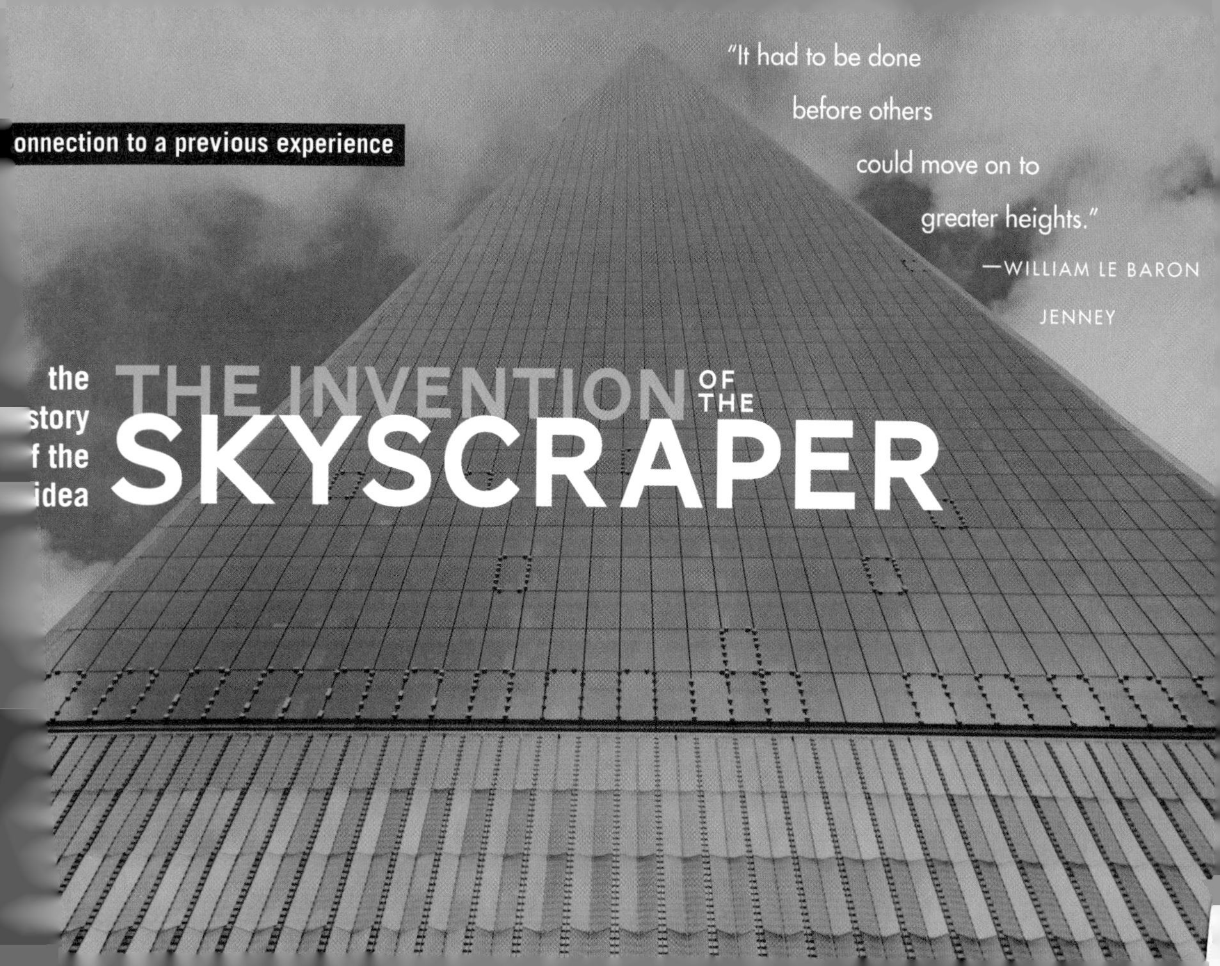

"It had to be done
before others
could move on to
greater heights."
—WILLIAM LE BARON JENNEY

the story f the idea

THE INVENTION OF THE SKYSCRAPER

58

Diagram It

Make a flowchart
for your project.
Can't do it?
At what point do
get hung up?
Is there a reason

One step
leads
to another.

PEOPLE HAVE ALWAYS HAD THE DESIRE TO GET HIGHER. During a visit to the Philippines as a teenager, William Le Baron Jenney noticed that the native huts were built of light, flexible bamboo frames that could withstand tropical storms. Years later, after becoming an architect, he needed a solution to build Chicago up instead of out. Thinking back to the bamboo huts, Jenney put the load of the building on a steel skeleton instead of the walls, which allowed buildings to be built higher. In 1885, Chicago's 10-story-high Home Insurance Building became the first building made with steel beam construction, and the first skyscraper.

59

Try It On

Commit to your idea for a day or two and see how it feels. If it doesn't go anywhere, throw it out or take a new direction.

Chuck Berry liked to try things out on stage to see how the audience would react. At the Cosmopolitan Club in St. Louis in 1953, when he was first defining his style, Berry added some country-western twangs into his blues guitar style to create "a unique hillbilly sound." The audience was stunned at first by this new sound, but soon everyone was trying to figure out how to dance to this new music that was eventually called rock 'n' roll.

Made from worn-out clothes, the quilts made by the women of Gee's Bend, Alabama, are examples of turning something ordinary into something extraordinary. Here's *Housetop* by Mary L. Bennett, circa 1965.

60

Recycle

Can an old or unused
idea be modified
slightly to work for
something else?

"There is no such thing as a new idea. It is impossible. We simply take a lot of old
ideas and put them into a sort of mental kaleidoscope. We give them a turn and they
make new and curious combinations." — MARK TWAIN, *Mark Twain's Own
Autobiography: The Chapters from the North American Review*

Frank Lloyd Wright wanted the Guggenheim Museum to work in a different way from other museums. Instead of requiring visitors to exit the museum by retracing their steps back through galleries, Wright wanted to lead the visitor all the way through. Inspired by nature, he modeled his design on a nautilus shell, and this natural path allowed the museum to function in a new and unique way.

What Is Your Concept?

What is the "why" behind the idea?
Finish this sentence: *This exists because . . .*

What is your idea based on? Does it convey a new point of view? If you don't have a reason behind your idea, the project won't have depth and the idea may not be strong enough to last.

Practice thinking conceptually. Make up a concept for each mundane part of your daily routine. Your breakfast is about energy, brushing your teeth is about renewal, and your drive to work is the great journey.

THIS IS A
(RORSCHACH)
TEST

Hermann Rorschach got his idea for the Rorschach test
from the Swiss game called Klecksographie, or Blotto.
In this game, children created inkblots by dropping ink on paper,
folding it in half, and then unfolding it.
They then described what they saw in the interesting shapes or used them
as inspiration for making up poems and acting out charades.
How can you describe what you see?

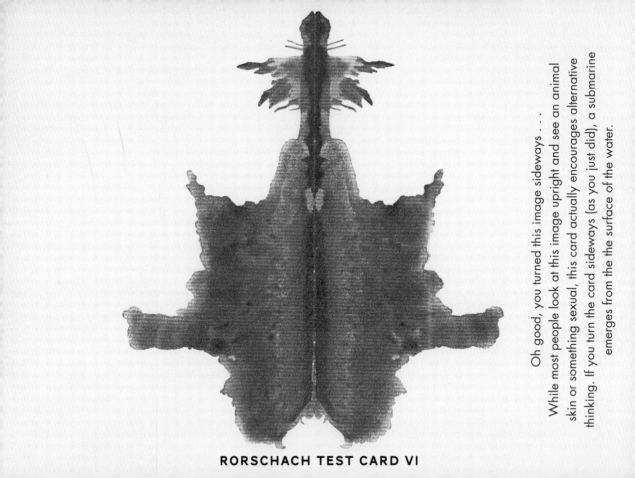

Oh good, you turned this image sideways . . .

While most people look at this image upright and see an animal skin or something sexual, this card actually encourages alternative thinking. If you turn the card sideways (as you just did), a submarine emerges from the the surface of the water.

RORSCHACH TEST CARD VI

All of the 26 capital letters you use every day
can be found in this structure.

When handwriting transitioned to stonecutting, letterforms needed to be simplified. The Greeks based each letterform on a simple geometric shape.

"[Artist] Albrecht Dürer and others followed its simple but rational logic: a circle within a square, the square subdivided into four squares with circles and half circles, ad infinitum."
— ROB CARTER, coauthor of *Typographic Design: Form and Communication*

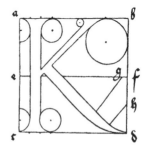

Do You Have a Structure?

Skeletons, architecture, layout grids, city plans, constellations, a spider web, a cell — everything works better and makes a little more sense because it is organized. Once you have the structure, you are free.

Elizabeth Gilbert used the *japa mala* necklace with its 108 prayer beads as the structure for her book *Eat, Pray, Love*. In Hinduism and Buddhism the number 108 is auspicious, a "perfect three-digit multiple of three," and represents supreme balance. "I have decided to structure it like a japa mala," said Gilbert, "dividing my story into 108 tales, or beads. This string of 108 tales is further divided into three sections about Italy, India and Indonesia — the three countries I visited during this year of self-inquiry. This division means that there are 36 tales in each section, which appeals to me on a personal level because I am writing all this during my thirty-sixth year."

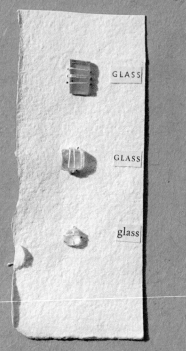

GLASS

GLASS

glass

glass

OTHER GLASSES

TUMBLER

TALL GLASS

ROCKS GLASS

Your categories only have to make sense to you.

Bookbinder Shoshannah Wineburg writes: "When you look down at a pile of broken glass or a crushed seed head, all the shards and seeds look the same. But I love how, when you pick up individual pieces and lay them out side by side, you recognize their differences, their unique qualities."

63

Categorize

It might help to organize the parts of your project into categories, like a grocery store and its aisles. Get yourself some different-colored notecards or folders, start a spreadsheet, draw a pie chart, fill the floor with boxes, or just write a list with different headings.

Even time has been categorized. Before the twentieth century, each town used to keep its own time, but as people started to move faster around the world on trains, this system became confusing. In 1876, Sir Sandford Fleming, a civil engineer tired of missing trains, proposed a fix. Fleming established Greenwich, England (zero degrees longitude), as standard time and divided the world into 24 time zones fanning out from that one point. Railroads adopted his system quickly, but the Standard Time Act wasn't put into effect until 1918.

THE INVENTION OF THE
PIE CHART

WILLIAM PLAYFAIR, a Scottish political economist, realized that when information was presented in tables, readers barely understood what they had read. He realized that if he presented the information more visually, in a line graph or bar chart, it could be more easily compared and was more memorable. In his 1801 publication *The Statistical Breviary*, Playfair designed a new chart comparing the revenues of the nations of Europe, depicting each country's land mass as a different size circle. For Turkey, because its empire spread over three continents, he had to break up the circle into three parts: green for Asia, red for Europe, and yellow for Africa — introducing the first pie chart.

This is what all
the fuss is about:

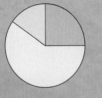

THIS
IS NOT A
(RORSCHACH)
TEST

How many different things can you see in this picture?

A brain? An onion?

Two amoebas? What else?

IF OPPORTUNITY

DOESN'T

KNOCK,

BUILD A DOOR.

— Milton Berle

Or just write your own personal mission statement.

Think about what word or sentence sums up what you'd like to achieve.

What kind of experience do you want to create?

64

Write a Mission Statement

Corporations use mission statements to define their goals and values for the customer, and nonprofits use them to define their purpose for donors. For an individual project, it really helps to have a statement or mantra in your head, on a napkin, or as a poster on the wall to keep you focused. It can be simple. For example, if you are designing a book about tomatoes, your statement might be, "I would like the book to feel warm, like a summer day."

In the business world, your mission is to state your U.S.P. (unique selling proposition).

"We help children realize their potential and build their futures. We nurture children and strengthen communities." — BIG BROTHERS BIG SISTERS

THE SAME
BUT DIFFERENT

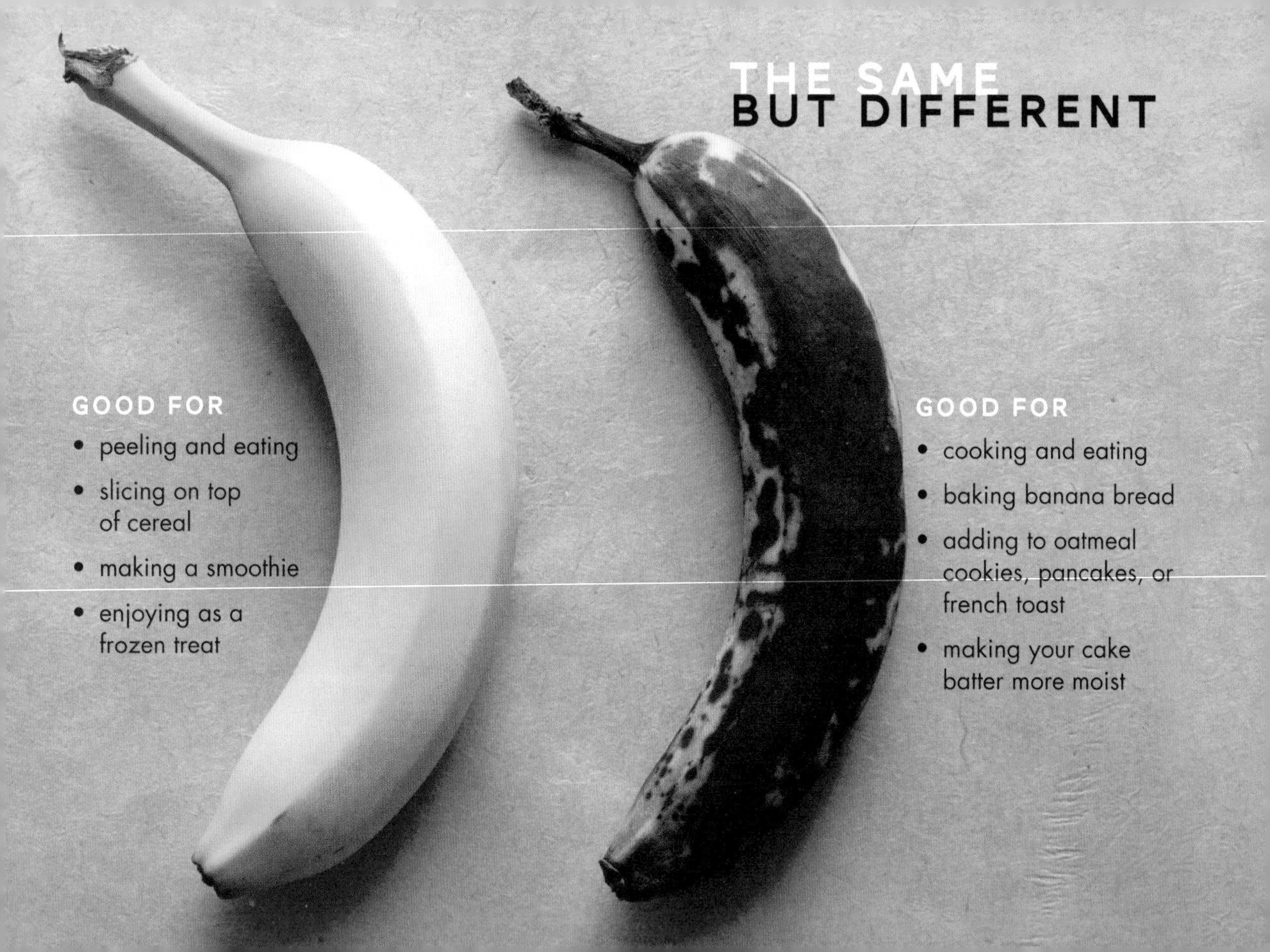

GOOD FOR

- peeling and eating
- slicing on top of cereal
- making a smoothie
- enjoying as a frozen treat

GOOD FOR

- cooking and eating
- baking banana bread
- adding to oatmeal cookies, pancakes, or french toast
- making your cake batter more moist

Compare/Contrast, Assess/Evaluate

So it turns out you aren't working in a vacuum: other people are thinking about the same thing. Time to research again. Now that you have a better idea of what you're doing, read everything about your topic and see what has been done before. Are there other versions of it? What are your first impressions of what's already out there? What makes your version necessary? What one thing can make it better?

Does something already exist?

☐ YES: What makes this thing good or bad?

☐ NO: Why not?

small goals
add up

Think Like a Marathon Runner

When training for a marathon, you have to set small, attainable goals for yourself every day.

"Goals form your roadmap to success. You won't get near your potential without having good goals. . . . Include an element of specificity: 'I want to run 30 seconds faster for 5K' instead of 'I want to run faster,' or 'I want to run 5 days a week' instead of 'I want to run more.'"

— MEB KEFLEZIGHI
2004 Olympic silver medalist and winner of the
2009 New York City Marathon and 2014 Boston Marathon

IS YOUR PROJECT BOLD, DYNAMIC, OR FUN ENOUGH?

Everything is so much more exciting if it makes a statement.
Make a statement loudly — a bold red dress,
a drum-roll entrance, some real fighting words.

It's about uncovering the right layer hiding beneath the surface. Detail of *Spiral 01*, by Maud Vantours

67

Think Like an Actor

Create a profile of your project as an actor does for a character when preparing for a role. What is your back story? Who is the project for? Why? Does it belong in the city or country? Is it one of a kind or part of a big family? Does it have a short or long past? What is its purpose?

In an interview with Roger Ebert, Meryl Streep describes the background work she did to learn about Karen Silkwood's life in order to play her in the movie *Silkwood*:

"Basically what I figured out is that everybody has a different impression of you. Your lover, mother, co-worker, all have these varying and contradictory impressions, and what you get is not the portrait of one person, but of three or four."

— MERYL STREEP,
as told to Roger Ebert

68

No More Country Music Videos

Be less literal. Try to give the audience more information in a unique way. Show or tell, but not both.

A story called "Lost Truck" with a picture of a truck doesn't make the reader pause or think. Instead of showing what you say, show what was left behind: tire tracks in the sand.

Keep an Open Mind

Even after the initial idea is formed, realize that it could always be better. Don't assume that you've got it right or that the outcome will be exactly what you expect. If you are not open to other opinions or possibilities, you might miss out on the opportunity to improve.

In an episode of Garry Marshall's TV series *The Odd Couple*, Felix Unger says, "When you assume, you make an *ASS* out of *U* and *ME*." But Thomas Edison was way ahead of him. When he took a potential new research candidate out to lunch, if the interviewee seasoned his soup before trying it, the interview was over. Edison didn't want to work with people who would assume anything — even about properly seasoned soup.

Cloud, Cloud, Manhattan from the *Pictures of Cloud* series, 2002
Art © Vik Muniz/Licensed by VAGA, New York, NY

In 2001 Vik Muniz wanted to give New Yorkers another reason to look up at the sky. Working with a crop-dusting airplane, Muniz created a series of cloud outlines. "The watching of clouds, whether as a method of forecasting or a form of amusement has been going on for centuries: what one person sees as a chariot, another may see as a bear or as a gathering of angels. Visualization comes from within the observer."

— VIK MUNIZ

70

Try It Out

Pin it up at the office or on a telephone pole, or put it online.

What happens when people see it, do it, or use it?

If they don't respond, why didn't they?

Be objective: Do you like it? Would you actually buy it?

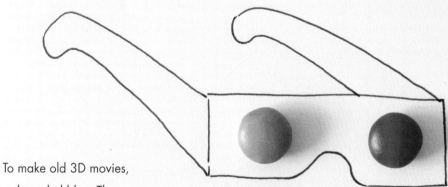

To make old 3D movies,
red needed blue. The
colored filters let red
light in through your left
eye, and blue light in
through your right eye.
Your brain did the rest.

71

Maybe You Need a Partner

Look for someone who has different skills that complement your own. Maybe he or she has a car to drive you somewhere you need to go. Maybe you just need to let go and delegate. Let someone else take over for a while, and give the project a new direction.

YIN/YANG • BREAD/BUTTER • BATMAN/ROBIN

COOKIE/MILK • FRED/GINGER • SALT/PEPPER

BEN/JERRY • PEANUT BUTTER/JELLY • HANSEL/

GRETEL • THUNDER/LIGHTNING • FISH/CHIPS

PENN/TELLER • EGGS/BACON • THELMA/LOUISE

HAMBURGER/FRIES • JACK/JILL • SOUP/SALAD

JEKYLL/HYDE • CHIPS/DIP • STARSKY/HUTCH

HAMMER/NAIL • LEWIS/CLARK • OIL/VINEGAR

A beautiful movie star and a composer met at a dinner party and invented a "secret communication system." Huh?

Hedy Lamarr (Hedy Kiesler Markey on their patent) loved math and tinkering. She was also a good listener — and learned a lot about military technology when her first husband, Friedrich Mandl, was talking at parties with Hitler and Mussolini. George Antheil was an avant-garde composer who became famous for his score for Fernand Léger's 1924 abstract film *Ballet Mécanique*. When the two met in 1940, their conversation turned to radio-controlled torpedoes (naturally), and Hedy realized that they were "talking and changing frequencies" as they spoke. Hedy's idea of frequency hopping and

Antheil's ability to synchronize rapidly changing radio frequencies evolved into a patent for the torpedo guidance system — which eventually inspired GPS, Wi-Fi, and Bluetooth technology.

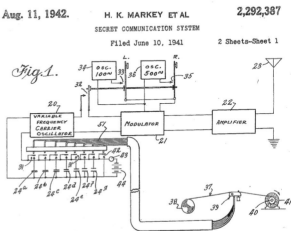

the story of the idea

THE INVENTION OF WIRELESS TECHNOLOGY

Here is Claude Chappe's telegraph tower from 1870. Using signaling arms that moved with ropes and pulleys, operators could send semaphore messages to other stations.

ALL FOR ONE (GOAL), ONE (GOAL) FOR ALL — FASTER, BETTER COMMUNICATION

It started in ancient China, Eqypt, and Greece with drumbeats and smoke signals, and then:

1747   Benjamin Franklin establishes that electricity can move through air.

1790s   Semaphore signaling develops.

1800   Alessandro Volta invents the battery.

1826   André-Marie Ampère proves that electric current produces a magnetic field.

1831   Michael Faraday builds the direct-current generator to generate electricity.

1830s   Sir William Cooke and Sir Charles Wheatstone develop a telegraph system for railroad signaling in England.

1830s   Samuel Morse, Leonard Gale, and Alfred Vail produce a single-circuit telegraph that sends an electric signal across a wire to a receiver.

1844   Samuel B. Morse sends first Morse code message.

1873   James Clerk Maxwell publishes *A Treatise on Electricity and Magnetism*, which describes the movement of electromagnetic waves through space.

1878   David E. Hughes transmits signals with a clockwork keyed transmitter.

1887   Henrich Rudolf Hertz invents the oscillator and proves the existence of electromagnetic waves.

1891   Nikola Tesla demonstrates electro-magnetic induction (energy moving between two points without wire).

1895   Guglielmo Marconi sends the first radio telegraph transmission.

Radio led to television, cordless phones, GPS devices, cellphones, wireless networking and an industry that is still quickly growing and innovating based on one person's discoveries helping another's.

Get crackin'.

72 Get to Work

Think, erase, re-do. Work and then rework. Just get busy, because it's not going to get done by itself.

In 1817 in upstate New York, farmers were optimistic that the new Erie Canal project would bring more prosperity to their farms, but they were frustrated when progress was slow. The local men took matters into their own hands and developed tools and even cement to keep the canal construction moving forward. "All of these engineering improvisations by untrained talent would one day be known as Yankee ingenuity." — CHUCK FRIDAY, *Low Bridge; Everybody Down!*

In 1957, while working to develop a new type of textured wallpaper, Alfred W. Fielding and Marc Chavannes tried trapping air bubbles between two plastic shower curtains. It failed as wallpaper. They then tried it as insulation for a greenhouse and failed again. In 1959 IBM introduced the 1401 computer which needed to be packed and shipped carefully — and bubble wallpaper finally found its calling as Bubble Wrap, the packing material.

Fail

73

"Stumbles loom rather large, the more I write. . . . But they're very important. It's like hitting the wrong note. You have to do something else. . . . You have to make something out of that error, do a really powerfully creative thing."

— TONI MORRISON

Failure is painful, but totally necessary. Usually you learn more through failure than through success. It also might reveal what needs to be fixed in order to move forward and try again. Isolate what caused the failure, and attack only that problem first. Also, remember, you're not alone: you can learn from other people's failures as they will learn from yours.

74 Is It Time to Throw in the Towel?

Try giving up for a day or two.
Do you feel relief? Then the project wasn't right.
Itching to get back at it? Maybe it still has legs . . .

J. K. Rowling's little story about Harry Potter was rejected by publishers dozens of times. It came as a shock to Rowling, then, when the Bloomsbury CEO's eight-year-old daughter fell in love with the story and it was finally published.

too much to think about

much easier

shrink it

Try thinking about only a tiny part of the problem.
Instead of writing the Great American Novel, write about one day
in one character's life. Instead of tackling world peace,
find a way to improve communication in your workplace.
The small solution could lead to a larger one.

or crop it

Use one small part of what you already have.
Does it work better if it's cut in half? Or in quarters?

"**Encouragement seems to be the key. . . .**
There is evidence from neuroscience. The reptilian part of our brain, which sits in the center of our brain, when it's threatened, it shuts down the prefrontal cortex, the parts which learn, it shuts all of that down. Punishment and examinations are seen as threats. . . . We need to shift that balance back from threat to pleasure." — SUGATA MITRA, professor of Educational Technology at the School of Education, Newcastle University, England

"Make it work." — TIM GUNN, *Project Runway*

76

Critique

TIPS FOR GIVING FEEDBACK TO OTHERS

- Remember, it's about the whole, but it's also about the parts.
- Be constructive. Be objective. Be genuine.
- Find one thing to fix.
- Inspire them to move forward.
- Give praise where it's due.

Take a break and give the project some time to rest. When you go back to it, lay it out on the floor or tack it to the wall and look at it from a distance. Listen to it in another room or outside. Is it different enough? Is it creative enough? What would make it more interesting, either to you or to a different audience? To a fireman? To a brain surgeon? To someone from another country? What needs to be changed? Anything?

the
story
of the
idea

THE INVENTION OF THE
BAGLESS
VACUUM

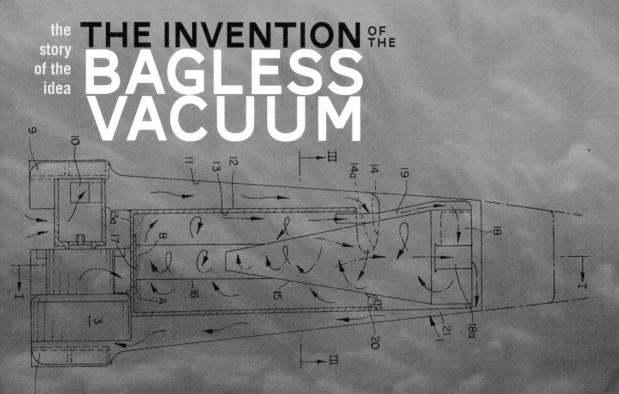

JAMES DYSON, AN INDUSTRIAL DESIGNER, WAS FRUSTRATED.

His Hoover Junior vacuum wasn't cleaning his house. Instead of sucking up dirt, the vacuum's bag kept getting clogged and just pushed the dust around the floor. Then he remembered a recent visit to an industrial sawmill where he had seen a cyclonic separator removing dust from the air. Could it be adapted to a smaller scale? It took five years and 5,127 prototypes before Dyson could finally clean his house better. His new, bright pink, dual-cyclone bagless "G-Force" vacuum cleaner was launched in 1983, but it wasn't until he won a 1991 International Design Fair award in Japan that his invention took off.

Because Dyson gets excited about trying to design things better — and enjoys inspiring creative problem-solving in others — he created the James Dyson Foundation in 2002 to encourage students to make mistakes and think differently.

77

Stop

Does it work?
Are you happy with
the result?
Then you're done . . .

until you think
of another way to
improve it.

THE STORY OF THE BOOK

I wish someone had given me all their secrets long ago —
so now I'm giving away mine.

I've always had a lot of ideas. In elementary school, my friends Amy and Mary and I formed the Inventions to Save the World Club. We made a tree fort without nails (it failed), invented a ventilation system (a fan) to eliminate pollution from smokestacks (didn't really know how to execute that one), and used car seat springs as our new energy shoes (not as bouncy as you might think). Okay, so they weren't exactly all good ideas, but I learned that if I kept thinking and was open to anything, I would generate more and more ideas, some better than the first.

In the past two years, I've had opportunities to meet and work with a lot of different students. During short portfolio reviews, working day to day as a mentor to two young designers, and helping with a photography/book class at Amherst College, I found that the same theme kept coming up: the students wanted to know how to move their ideas forward, but sometimes they just didn't know how to begin, continue, or finish. I wanted to try to show them the "how." My responses, whether design related or not, came back to the same things — learning to recognize what's in front of you and learning to see things from a new perspective. I started to think about ways I could help them look at their problems and concepts from different angles. Before I knew it, I was on the side of the road writing iPhone notes (I have a long drive to work), scribbling on sticky notes at all hours of the day, writing on magazine insert cards, all just to get the thoughts down quickly before they evaporated. I really didn't know why I needed to write it all down, I just knew I had to clear the flood of thoughts from my head. Within a few days I had a list, then a structure, which led to this book.

It was only after I had written everything down that I looked around to see what had been written on this subject before. It turns out there is a lot. Creative people problem-solve their whole lives, so it makes sense that we all arrive at similar methods. I also found that great scientific minds have done detailed studies and written many books on the subject of creativity, but very few have approached the subject visually. Images reveal another way in.

There is a process to developing ideas and thinking creatively, and there are steps you can take to help move that process along. I wanted to show, through examples from many different sources, how you can make connections that will help you start looking at information in a new way. Everyone doesn't have to become an artist, but everyone can be more observant. And you can train yourself to be better at anything, if you have an interest. Being creative is just about connecting thoughts you didn't put together before, and developing skills you didn't realize you had.

In one of the final scenes in the eighties movie *Working Girl*, Melanie Griffith's character, Tess, explains that her brilliant business merger idea was inspired by a tabloid newspaper's society pages — a highbrow idea coming from a lowbrow source. It's kind of perfect. There is no right or best way to get ideas. But the more open you are to possibility, and the more you observe, listen, read, talk to people, and travel (even just down the block), the more connections you'll make. And one idea leads to another . . .

— C. E.

Acknowledgments

This book is an accumulation of years of work and a lot of people's influence, so thank you to all — with a few extra notes below: Of course, a giant thank-you to all of the funny, smart, creative people at Storey who make it fun to go to work every day. To Michaela Jebb and Jeff Stiefel, who asked the questions that inspired me to start to write the answers down.

To Alethea Morrison, who gave me the opportunity to work with young designers, which started me thinking in a new way. To Mars Vilaubi, for his photographic knowledge and patience. To Jen Travis for her charm and organizational skills. And especially to Hannah Fries with her poetic wisdom and making me look better than I am, and Deborah Balmuth for her enthusiastic optimism when I presented her with this crazy list and pile of papers.

To Justin Kimball for asking me to contribute to his photography/book class at Amherst College, *Eight People, One Place* — the students were so sharp, talented, and curious, they inspired me to start writing frantically on Post-it notes.

To my carpool mates: Leslie Charles, Carleen Madigan, and Pam Thompson, who taught me about marathon running, writing, quilting, soccer, cooking, and gardening on our long drives. And thank you, Pam, for telling me to "just keep going."

To Tim Gunn for setting a fabulous example of what a mentor should be: honest, supportive, enthusiastic, and constructive.

To Hans Teensma, whose design firm Impress, Inc., provided the start of my book design career and provided 11 circles every week.

To the *Wondertime* staff — it was fast and furious and a really fun think tank. To Jeff Wagenheim for his brilliant "mind-expanding" 11 circle comment.

And a huge thank-you to all of the fabulous people who contributed 11 circles to this project. You've inspired me and taught me new ways to observe.

To my family: To my parents, for their support, and for paying for me to go to art school even though it "seemed weird." To my sister Susanne, who provided enthusiastic and constructive feedback for this book at the beginning, and who coined the term "the story of the idea." To my sister Jennifer and her Crotty family, who gave me a home when I worked in New York City, and to my brother Brian, who contributed one of my first 11 circle submissions.

To my husband, Dana, and our sons, Marty and Roy — the most loving and supportive, funniest, most creative men I know.

THE STORY _{OF THE} LIST

Your Idea Starts Here is full of facts, processes, and tips I have figured out in the course of life and during my years as a designer. Many smart people had many of these thoughts out in the world already, so here are some resources and a few of the stories behind these ideas.

Title Page: Illustration sketch by Phil Hackett (left). Paperclip submarine inspired by the work of Javier Perez.

"Fresh Ideas" Photograph: "The inspiration for the BIG SALE! series came from a photo of a supermarket in Martin Parr's collection Boring Postcards USA. I stumbled upon it while I was trying to come up with a way of advertising our new gallery, which had more windows than wall space. I think the thing that appealed to me was its utter simplicity and familiarity. Most artists these days tend to treat nostalgia like a four-letter word, but I'm not afraid to admit I have it. I often feel that I was born much too late . . . " — Michael McKay/ Empty Set Projects

Gather/Break/Build:
After I wrote my list of ways to generate ideas, I realized that the points fell into three categories: gathering your research and ideas, breaking down what you found into what you need, and building the idea into something you want.

2. Pick One Thing. Postcard: "I started embroidering postcards because I enjoyed the tactile recreation of idly passing the time in passive productivity. Altering each uniquely and exhibiting them in batches, I found that eventually themes arose — like in this one, where the pattern and color immerses itself in its monochromatic surroundings." — Shaun Kardinal

The Story of the Idea: For each of these "stories," I chose items on the theme of basic human needs: food, clothing, shelter, health, work, and the pursuit of happiness.

Windshield Wiper: Quotes from US patent no. 743,801, Window-Cleaning Device, and from the letter to Mary Anderson from Dinning & Eckenstein (Birmingham Public Library). You can look up any US patent here: uspto.gov. It's fascinating.

5. Think Like a Fashion Designer.
I worked at Condé Nast for Fairchild Books and got to research photography in their fabulous photo collection. Some of my favorite images were the fashion designers' photo inspirations for their collections.

8. Make a Connection. My sons play this game with each other all the time when we hike. They call it "hashtag." **Leonardo Ulian on his technological mandala series:** "I am intrigued by the fact that electronic technology has become an important part of our daily lives, almost something to worship. My technological mandalas are created by welding together electronic components of various shapes and colors in order to create an organized design that recalls figures of traditional mandalas. With this series I wanted to show what has been hidden from the eyes of the consumer, representing electronic circuits as extraordinary objects where the perfection of their design becomes something almost ethereal. Electronic technology is in a way impermanent, and is constantly changing and can become easily obsolete, like the traditional sand mandalas can be easily brushed away after days of work."

Stethoscope: Quotes from *A Treatise on the Diseases of the Chest and on Mediate Auscultation* by R.T.H. Laënnec, M.D., translated from the third French Edition, with copious notes, by John Forbes, M.D. F.R.S.

11. You Can't Have It. For some insight on the inspiration behind his cooking, see Oprah's interview with Jean-Georges Vongerichten in *O* magazine, August 2015.

13,14. Play to Your Strengths, Exploit a Weakness. While at *Wondertime* magazine, my coworkers and I all took the Myers-Briggs test, which explained everyone's strengths . . . and weaknesses. If you want to see who you are, visit myersbriggs.org.

17. Look to Other Cultures and Traditions. For more information on Japanese influences on Monet and Wright, see "How Japan's Art Inspired the West," by Jeff Michael Hammond in the *Japan Times*, and William Cronon's essay "Inconstant Unity: The Passion of Frank Lloyd Wright" in *Frank Lloyd Wright, Architect*, published by the Museum of Modern Art.

18. Look to Other Fields of Study. To see more galleries of work from the Art of Science competition, go to: artofsci.princeton.edu/.

19. Change Your Routine. If you want to make a line drawing like Julianna Kunstler's, visit the tutorial on her website: juliannakunstler.com.

20, 21. Brainstorm Light/Brainstorm Bold. *Wondertime* magazine was a startup, and we brainstormed a lot to come up with story and art ideas. I was an introvert in a room of extroverts, and it was only later (especially after reading Susan Cain's book *Quiet*) that I figured out some ways that brainstorming might have been more productive for me.

24. Get Emotional. I heard Cesar Kuriyama on the TED Radio Hour, and at that time he had recorded himself one second a day for four years and four months. Check out the 1 Second Everyday app or his website, cesarkuriyama.com.

25. Shuffle Papers. Catalina Viejo Lopez de Roda says about her work, "Like [my] paintings and drawings, the collages are extremely personal. They adhere to the same rules of divisions and layering, but offer a different perspective. I can recall where I have found every piece of paper, and I hide information within them. . . . Each letter is aimed at a very specific being. Just like any letter, I think about what I want to say and who I am saying it to. I create a psychological portrait in which I explore a personal dialogue and the feelings a specific subject generates within me."

29. Don't Overlook the Obvious. Color blindness test created by Dr. J. J. Creamer. "This test was developed because of the need for an inexpensive color blindness test geared toward a nonreader or preschooler. Early detection of color blindness is key to making life adjustments." — Judith Creamer

30. Think Like an Optimist. Full disclosure: I am a delusional optimist. Listen to Amy Cuddy's TED talk, "Your Body Language Shapes Who You Are." And watch a video about Nobel winner Daniel Kahneman at inc.com.

What Is Your Super Power?: Answer courtesy of Marty Gentes.

31. Train Like a Spy. In the FX show *The Americans*, Keri Russell's character, Elizabeth, has to train a young spy. The training involves sharpening his observation skills while walking down the block — then telling her what everyone was wearing, reading, and doing on that street.

35. Stop Whatever You're Doing. This is a design trick. It doesn't work in white? Try black. Edward de Bono coined the term *lateral thinking* to describe this technique and published a book by that name in 1970.

37. Limit Your Options. I learned about *jugaad* from Navi Radjou's interview during the TED Radio Hour. See his talk at TED.com.

38. Deconstruct. Text for Laura Didyk's artwork from "Mother Tongue," by Lauren Collins from the *New Yorker*, November 4, 2013.

39. Not Getting the Idea Across? This is a softer way of saying what my RISD typography professor, Franz Werner, would say (in a Swiss-German accent) during critiques if he didn't like someone's work: "Zisss . . . zisss is shit."

40. Rearrange and Restructure. I saw the Bosnian movie *Before the Rain* when it came out and loved that it was a triptych, shown out of order in a circular structure instead of a linear one. It just so happens that Quentin Tarantino was making *Pulp Fiction* in the same way at the same time — an example of simultaneous creative thinking. **From the artist William Smith on his (and Anonymous's) Exquisite Corpse drawing:** "As an introduction to wet media, my students and I play a round of the surrealist game the Exquisite Corpse to alleviate some of the anxiety of drawing with pen and ink. Aside from its playful nature, there are many benefits of playing this game. First, it exposes students to art history. Second, it is a collaborative process. And third, it is an unorthodox approach to image making, which encourages exploration and acceptance of an unknown outcome."

42. Now Screw Up Like a Scientist. Sam Gershman is at Harvard now, teaching in the Department of Psychology and Center for Brain Science.

44. Try Mozart. *The Mozart Effect: Tapping the Power of Music to Heal the Body, Strengthen the Mind, and Unlock the Creative Spirit*, by Don Campbell.

45. Shape/Size/Proportion/Color. Edison quote from Michael Michalko's "Thomas Edison's Creative Thinking Habits", on thinkjarcollective.com.

47. Look Back. For more information on how the Founding Fathers drew from Iroquois principles, see John H. Lienhard's article "The Iroquois and the U.S. Government, Native American Contributions," uh.edu/engines/epi709.htm, and Bruce E. Johansen's book *Forgotten Founders: How the American Indian Helped Shape Democracy.*

48. Talk with a Friend. Albert Einstein's discussion was recorded by Ishiwara (who took notes in Japanese) during Einstein's lecture in Kyoto on December 14, 1922. **In regard to her artwork,** Lisa Hochstein says, "Working in collage allows me to bring together disparate fragments from the world outside my studio. In this series I've limited my materials as I explore subtle variations in the positioning of two simple geometric forms."

50. Share Your Idea. Susanna Bauer writes that her work "pays homage to nature as well as holding up a mirror to the viewer. Constructed with dry leaves and cotton yarn the pieces hold a fine balance of fragility and strength reflecting individual stories and connections."

Fortune Cookie: After becoming frustrated because his fortune cookie didn't reveal a real prediction, Dana Gentes wrote these alternative fortunes.

53. Take a Walk. I read about Nietzsche and Kant and their walking habits in Shane Parrish's article "A Philosophy of Walking: Thoreau, Nietzsche and Kant on Walking" at farnamstreetblog. com, which led me to *A Philosophy of Walking* by Frederic Gros, and *Wanderlust: A History of Walking* by Rebecca Solnit.

55. Now Wait. When I wait in line for coffee I find it really interesting just to stand still while everyone rushes around me. I've learned to embrace the wait. **Javier Perez says of his art,** "My work is very simple and minimal. I want people to be able to take a break from the saturation of photos in general.

My motto: Create every day. No matter your skills."

56. Take a Break. "The Incubation Effect: Hatching a Solution?" is the title of the study by Sophie Ellwood, Gerry Pallier, Allan Snyder, and Jason Gallate from the Centre for the Mind, University of Sydney, Australia.

57. Go to Sleep. I've learned from many all-nighters that two hours of sleep makes you more productive the next day than no sleep at all. When I heard Russell Foster's explanation in his TED talk, "Why Do We Sleep?" it all made sense.

61. What Is Your Concept? Learn more about the Frank Lloyd Wright building at guggenheim.org.

63. Categorize. Bookbinder and designer Shoshannah Wineburg writes about her glass samples: "I began collecting all sorts of small detritus on my walks: seeds, glass, shells, pebbles. I enjoy playing with the labels, seeing how type styles, sizes, weight can add descriptive properties to the same word. Look closer; notice the individual nature of the smallest things around you."

68. No More Country Music Videos. I thought of this line when trying to describe the kind of photography we didn't want at *Wondertime*. In some older country music videos, if "he's walkin' out the door," they showed the guy walking out the door. If we could show a different perspective or angle on the story, the feature would be more interesting to the reader. I recently saw Chip Kidd's TED talk in which he explains that his graphic design professor told the class on the first day that you either show the apple or write the word *apple*, but don't do both, because your audience deserves better. That could have saved me some thinking time.

71. Maybe You Need a Partner. Hedy Lamarr was a fascinating person with a fascinating life. Read about her at HedyLamarr.com. See also "If it wasn't for Hedy Lamarr, we wouldn't have Wi-Fi." *The Guardian*, December 4, 2011.

73. Fail. An Interview with Toni Morrison by Rebecca Gross for *NEA Arts Magazine.*

76. Critique. Encouragement quote from Sugata Mitra's TED talk, "Build a School in the Cloud."

the 11-circle challenge

Now that you have so many ways to jump-start creative thinking, it's time to show off your skills. In the creative spirit of this book, and as an experiment in limiting criteria, I started a blog: 11circles.tumblr.com. Contributors (that means you!) are invited to submit 11 circles. There are no other rules.

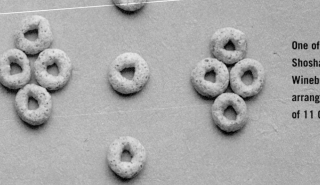

One of Shoshannah Wineburg's arrangements of 11 Cheerios

The endsheets of this book show details from submissions to the 11 Circles blog. See the whole collection and submit your own 11 circles here: 11circles.tumblr.com.

Writer Kevin Markey takes us around the world. When entered into Google Earth, the sets of geographic coordinates he submitted reveal satellite images of 11 earthly rings. The tour includes famous landmarks that hold special memories for Markey (Stonehenge, Rome's Circus Maximus) as well as personal touchstones, from the sixth-century Irish settlement that inspired his name (St. Kevin's Glendalough) to places he has studied, worked, and lived. The journey finishes with the circle at the end of his street, because sometimes the best part of a trip is coming home. Here, he brings us to Paris.

© luke jaeger

© trisha thompson

© michèle coppin

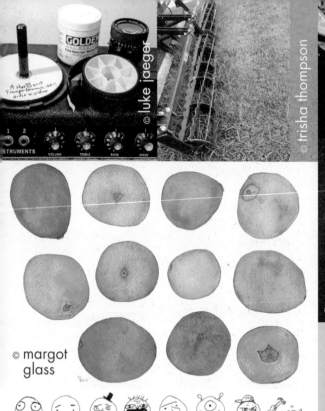

© margot glass

© marty gentes

Rest In Peace #12

© ann hallock (11 books that influenced her life)

LET'S GO:
The Budget Guide to
EUROPE
1990

© dave gloman

© emily spiegelman